VALLEJO HIGH SCHOOL

The Underdogs

and Related Readings

McDougal Littell
A HOUGHTON MIFFLIN COMPANY

Evanston, Illinois   *Boston*   *Dallas*

Acknowledgments

Viking Penguin: Excerpt from "Zapata: A Narrative, in Dramatic Form, of the Life of Emiliano Zapata" and excerpt from *Viva Zapata!;* both excerpts from *Zapata* by John Steinbeck, edited by Robert Morsberger. Copyright © 1975 by Elaine Steinbeck and The Viking Press Inc. Reprinted by permission of Viking Penguin, a division of Penguin Books USA Inc.

University of California Press: "The Festival of Bullets" by Martín Luis Guzmán, from *The Spanish American Short Story: A Critical Anthology,* edited by Seymour Menton; Copyright © 1980 by The Regents of the University of California. Reprinted by permission of The University of California Press.

Robert Bly: "The Dictators" by Pablo Neruda, from *Neruda and Vallejo: Selected Poems,* edited by Robert Bly, Beacon, Boston, 1971, 1993; Copyright © 1971, 1993 by Robert Bly. Reprinted with the permission of Robert Bly.

Routledge, Inc., New York and Reed Consumer Books Ltd.: "When Evil-Doing Comes Like Falling Rain" from *Bertolt Brecht: 1913–1956,* edited by John Willett and Ralph Manheim; Copyright © 1976 by Eyre Methuen Ltd. Reprinted by permission of Routledge, Inc., N.Y. and Reed Consumer Books Ltd.

Leon Clark: "'It's Terrible' or 'It's Fine'" by Mao Zedong, from *Through Chinese Eyes,* edited by Leon Clark (New York: CITE Books, The Council on International and Public Affairs, 1988), pp. 39–42. Reprinted by permission of Leon Clark.

The Rosen Publishing Group, Inc.: "Tienanmen Square: A Soldier's Story" by Xiao Ye, from *Teenage Soldiers, Adult Wars.* Reprinted by permission of the Rosen Publishing Group, Inc.

Cover illustration by Michael Steirnagle.

ISBN 0-395-79679-2

234567—DCI—02 01 00 99 98 97 96

Contents

Continued

The Underdogs

A Novel of the Mexican Revolution

Mariano Azuela

Translated by

E. Munguía, Jr.

Part One

....

"How beautiful the revolution! Even in its most barbarous aspect it is beautiful," Solís said with deep feeling.

Chapter 1

"That's no animal, I tell you! Listen to the dog barking! It *must* be a human being."

The woman stared into the darkness of the sierra.

"What if they're soldiers?" said a man, who sat Indian-fashion, eating, a coarse earthenware plate in his right hand, three folded tortillas in the other.

The woman made no answer, all her senses directed outside the hut. The beat of horses' hoofs rang in the quarry nearby. The dog barked again, louder and more angrily.

"Well, Demetrio, I think you had better hide, all the same."

Stolidy, the man finished eating; next he reached for a *cántaro* and gulped down the water in it; then he stood up.

"Your rifle is under the mat," she whispered.

A tallow candle illumined the small room. In one corner stood a plow, a yoke, a goad, and other agricultural implements. Ropes hung from the roof, securing an old adobe mold, used as a bed; on it a child slept, covered with gray rags.

Demetrio buckled his cartridge belt about his waist and picked up his rifle. He was tall and well built, with a sanguine face and beardless chin; he wore shirt and trousers of white cloth, a broad Mexican hat and leather sandals.

With slow, measured step, he left the room, vanishing into the impenetrable darkness of the night.

The dog, excited to the point of madness, had jumped over the corral fence.

Suddenly a shot rang out. The dog moaned, then barked no more. Some men on horseback rode up, shouting and swearing; two of them dismounted, while the other hung back to watch the horses.

"Hey, there, woman: we want food! Give us eggs, milk, beans, anything you've got! We're starving!"

"Curse the sierra! It would take the Devil himself not to lose his way!"

"Guess again, Sergeant! Even the Devil would go astray if he were as drunk as you are."

The first speaker wore chevrons on his arm, the other red stripes on his shoulders.

"Whose place is this, old woman? Or is it an empty house? God's truth, which is it?"

"Of course it's not empty. How about the light and that child there? Look here, confound it, we want to eat, and damn quick too! Are you coming out or are we going to make you?"

"You swine! Both of you! You've gone and killed my dog, that's what you've done! What harm did he ever do you? What did you have against *him?*"

The woman reentered the house, dragging the dog behind her, very white and fat, with lifeless eyes and flabby body.

"Look at those cheeks, Sergeant! Don't get riled, light of my life: I swear I'll turn your home into a dovecot, see?"

"By God!" he said, breaking off into song:

"Don't look so haughty, dear,
Banish all fears,
Kiss me and melt to me,
I'll drink up your tears!"
His alcoholic tenor trailed off into the night.

"Tell me what they call this ranch, woman?" the sergeant asked.

"Limón," the woman replied curtly, carrying wood to the fire and fanning the coals.

"So we're in Limón, eh, the famous Demetrio

Macías' country, eh? Do you hear that, Lieutenant? We're in Limón."

"Limón? What the hell do I care? If I'm bound for hell, Sergeant, I might as well go there now. I don't mind, now that I've found as good a remount as this! Look at the cheeks on the darling, look at them! There's a pair of ripe red apples for a fellow to bite into!"

"I'll wager you know Macías the bandit, lady? I was in the pen with him at Escobedo, once."

"Bring me a bottle of tequila, Sergeant: I've decided to spend the night with this charming lady. . . . What's that? The colonel? . . . Why in God's name talk about the colonel now? He can go straight to hell, for all I care. And if he doesn't like it, it's all right with me. Come on, Sergeant, tell the corporal outside to unsaddle the horses and feed them. I'll stay here all night. Here, my girl, you let the sergeant fry the eggs and warm up the tortillas; you come here to me. See this wallet full of nice new bills? They're all for you, darling. Sure, I want you to have them. Figure it out for yourself. I'm drunk, see: I've a bit of a load on and that's why I'm kind of hoarse, you might call it. I left half my gullet down Guadalajara way, and I've been spitting the other half out all the way up here. Oh well, who cares? But I want you to have that money, see, dearie? Hey, Sergeant, where's my bottle? Now, little girl, come here and pour yourself a drink. You won't, eh? Aw, come on! Afraid of your—er—husband . . . or whatever he is, huh? Well, if he's skulking in some hole, you tell him to come out. What the hell do I care? I'm not scared of rats, see!"

Suddenly a white shadow loomed on the threshold.

"Demetrio Macías!" the sergeant cried as he stepped back in terror.

The lieutenant stood up, silent, cold and motionless as a statue.

"Shoot them!" the woman croaked.

"Oh, come, you'll surely spare us! I didn't know you were there. I'll always stand up for a brave man."

Demetrio stood his ground, looking them up and down, an insolent and disdainful smile wrinkling his face.

"Yes, I not only respect brave men, but I like them. I'm proud and happy to call them friends. Here's my hand on it: friend to friend." Then, after a pause: "All right, Demetrio Macías, if you don't want to shake hands, all right! But it's because you don't know me, that's why, just because the first time you saw me I was doing this dog's job. But look here, I ask you, what in God's name can a man do when he's poor and has a wife to support and kids? . . . Right you are, Sergeant, let's go: I've nothing but respect for the home of what I call a brave man, a real, honest, genuine man!"

When they had gone, the woman drew close to Demetrio.

"Holy Virgin, what agony! I suffered as though it was you they'd shot."

"You go to father's house, quick!" Demetrio ordered. She wanted to hold him in her arms; she entreated, she wept. But he pushed away from her gently and, in a sullen voice, said, "I've an idea the whole lot of them are coming."

"Why didn't you kill 'em?"

"Their hour hasn't struck yet."

They went out together; she bore the child in her arms. At the door, they separated, moving off in different directions.

The moon peopled the mountain with vague shadows. As he advanced at every turn of his way Demetrio could see the poignant, sharp silhouette of a woman pushing forward painfully, bearing a child in her arms.

When, after many hours of climbing, he gazed back, huge flames shot up from the depths of the canyon by the river. It was his house, blazing. . . .

Chapter 2

Everything was still swathed in shadows as Demetrio Macías began his descent to the bottom of the ravine. Between rocks striped with huge eroded cracks, and a squarely cut wall, with the river flowing below, a narrow ledge along the steep incline served as a mountain trail.

"They'll surely find me now and track us down like dogs," he mused. "It's a good thing they know nothing about the trails and paths up here. . . . But if they got someone from Moyahua to guide them . . ." He left the sinister thought unfinished. "All the men from Limón or Santa Rosa or the other nearby ranches are on our side: they wouldn't try to trail us. That *cacique* who's chased and run me ragged over these hills, is at Mohayua now; he'd give his eyeteeth to see me dangling from a telegraph pole with my tongue hanging out of my mouth, purple and swollen. . . ."

At dawn, he approached the pit of the canyon. Here, he lay on the rocks and fell asleep.

The river crept along, murmuring as the waters rose and fell in small cascades. Birds sang lyrically from their hiding among the *pitaya* trees. The monotonous, eternal drone of insects filled the rocky solitude with mystery.

Demetrio awoke with a start. He waded the river, following its course which ran counter to the canyon; he climbed the crags laboriously as an ant, gripping root and rock with his hands, clutching every stone in the trail with his bare feet.

When he reached the summit, he glanced down to see the sun steeping the valley in a lake of gold. Near the canyon, enormous rocks loomed protrudent, like fantastic Negro skulls. The *pitaya* trees rose tenuous, tall, like the tapering, gnarled fingers of a giant; other trees of all sorts bowed their crests toward the pit of the abyss. Amid the stark rocks and dry branches, roses bloomed like a white offering to the sun as smoothly, suavely, it unraveled its golden threads, one by one, from rock to rock.

Demetrio stopped at the summit. Reaching backward, with his right arm he drew his horn which hung at his back, held it up to his thick lips, and, swelling his cheeks out, blew three loud blasts. From across the hill close by, three sharp whistles answered his signal.

In the distance, from a conical heap of reeds and dry straws, man after man emerged, one after the other, their legs and chests naked, lambent and dark as old bronze. They rushed forward to greet Demetrio, and stopped before him, askance.

"They've burnt my house," he said.

A murmur of oaths, imprecations, and threats rose among them.

Demetrio let their anger run its course. Then he drew a bottle from under his shirt and took a deep swig; then he wiped the neck of the bottle with the back of his hand and passed it around. It passed from mouth to mouth; not a drop was left. The men passed their tongues greedily over their lips to recapture the tang of the liquor.

"Glory be to God and by His Will," said Demetrio, "tonight or tomorrow at the latest we'll meet the Federals. What do you say, boys, shall we let them find their way about these trails?"

The ragged crew jumped to their feet, uttering shrill cries of joy; then their jubilation turned sinister and they gave vent to threats, oaths and imprecations.

"Of course, we can't tell how strong they are," said Demetrio as his glance traveled over their faces in scrutiny.

"Do you remember Medina? Out there at Hostotipaquillo, he only had a half a dozen men with knives that they sharpened on a grindstone. Well, he held back the soldiers and the police, didn't he? And he beat them, too."

"We're every bit as good as Medina's crowd!" said a tall, broad-shouldered man with a black beard and bushy eyebrows.

"By God, if I don't own a Mauser and a lot of cartridges, if I can't get a pair of trousers and shoes, then my name's not Anastasio Montáñez! Look here, Quail, you don't believe it, do you? You ask my partner Demetrio if I haven't half a dozen bullets in me already. Christ! Bullets are marbles to me! And I dare you to contradict me!"

"Viva Anastasio Montáñez," shouted Manteca.

"All right, all right!" said Montáñez. "Viva Demetrio Macías, our chief, and long life to God in His heaven and to the Virgin Mary."

"Viva Demetrio Macías," they all shouted.

They gathered dry brush and wood, built a fire and placed chunks of fresh meat upon the burning coals. As the blaze rose, they collected about the fire, sat down Indian-fashion and inhaled the odor of the meat as it twisted on the crackling fire. The rays of the sun, falling about them, cast a golden radiance over the bloody hide of a calf, lying on the ground nearby. The meat dangled from a rope fastened to a *huizache* tree, to dry in the sun and wind.

"Well, men," Demetrio said, "you know we've only twenty rifles, besides my thirty-thirty. If there are just a few of them, we'll shoot until there's not a live man left. If there's a lot of 'em, we can give 'em a good scare, anyhow."

He undid a rag belt about his waist, loosened a knot in it and offered the contents to his companions. Salt. A murmur of approbation rose among them as each took a few grains between the tips of his fingers.

They ate voraciously; then, glutted, lay down on the ground, facing the sky. They sang monotonous, sad songs, uttering a strident shout after each stanza.

Chapter 3

In the brush and foliage of the sierra, Demetrio Macías and his threescore men slept until the halloo of the horn, blown by Pancracio from the crest of a peak, awakened them.

"Time, boys! Look around and see what's what!" Anastasio Montáñez said, examining his rifle springs. Yet he was previous; an hour or more elapsed with no sound or stir save the song of the locust in the brush or the frog stirring in his mudhole. At last, when the ultimate faint rays of the moon were spent in the rosy dimness of the dawn, the silhouette of a soldier loomed at the end of the trail. As they strained their eyes, they could distinguish others behind him, ten, twenty, a hundred. . . . Then, suddenly, darkness swallowed them up. Only when the sun rose, Demetrio's band realized that the canyon was alive with men, midgets seated on miniature horses.

"Look at 'em, will you?" said Pancracio. "Pretty, ain't they? Come on, boys, let's go and roll marbles with 'em."

Now the moving dwarf figures were lost in the dense chaparral, now they reappeared, stark and black against the ocher. The voices of officers, as they gave orders, and soldiers, marching at ease, were clearly audible.

Demetrio raised his hand; the locks of rifles clicked.

"Fire!" he cried tensely.

Twenty-one men shot as one; twenty-one soldiers fell off their horses. Caught by surprise, the column halted, etched like bas-reliefs in stone against the rocks.

Another volley and a score of soldiers hurtled down from rock to rock.

"Come out, bandits. Come out, you starved dogs!"

"To hell with you, you corn rustlers!"

"Kill the cattle thieves! Kill 'em!"

The soldiers shouted defiance to their enemies; the latter, giving proof of a marksmanship which had already made them famous, were content to keep under cover, quiet, mute.

"Look, Pancracio," said Meco, completely black save for his eyes and teeth. "This is for that man who passes that tree. I'll get the son of a . . ."

"Take that! Right in the head. You saw it, didn't you, mate? Now, this is for the fellow on the roan horse. Down you come, you shave-headed bastard!"

"I'll give that lad on the trail's edge a shower of lead. If you don't hit the river, I'm a liar! Now: look at him!"

"Oh, come on, Anastasio, don't be cruel; lend me your rifle. Come along, one shot, just one!"

Manteca and Quail, unarmed, begged for a gun as a boon, imploring permission to fire at least a shot apiece.

"Come out of your holes if you've got any guts!"

"Show your faces, you lousy cowards!"

From peak to peak, the shouts rang as distinctly as though uttered across a street. Suddenly, Quail stood up, naked, holding his trousers to windward as though he were a bullfighter flaunting a red cape, and the soldiers below the bull. A shower of shots peppered upon Demetrio's men.

"God! That was like a hornet's nest buzzing overhead," said Anastasio Montáñez, lying flat on the ground without daring to wink an eye.

"Here, Quail, you son of a bitch, you stay where I told you," roared Demetrio.

They crawled to take new positions. The soldiers, congratulating themselves on their successes, ceased firing when another volley roused them.

"More coming!" they shouted.

Some, panic-stricken, turned their horses back; others, abandoning their mounts, began to climb up the mountain and seek shelter behind the rocks. The officers had to shoot at them to enforce discipline.

"Down there, down there!" said Demetrio as he leveled his rifle at the translucent thread of the river.

A soldier fell into the water; at each shot, invariably a soldier bit the dust. Only Demetrio was shooting in that direction; for every soldier killed, ten or twenty of them, intact, climbed afresh on the other side.

"Get those coming up from under! *Los de Abajo!* Get the underdogs!" he screamed.

Now his fellows were exchanging rifles, laughing and making wagers on their marksmanship.

"My leather belt if I miss that head there, on the black horse!"

"Lend me your rifle, Meco."

"Twenty Mauser cartridges and a half yard of sausage if you let me spill that lad riding the bay mare. All right! Watch me. . . . There! See him jump! Like a bloody deer."

"Don't run, you half-breeds. Come along with you! Come and meet Father Demetrio!"

Now it was Demetrio's men who screamed insults. Manteca, his smooth face swollen in exertion, yelled his lungs out. Pancracio roared, the veins and muscles in his neck dilated, his murderous eyes narrowed to two evil slits.

Demetrio fired shot after shot, constantly warning his men of impending danger, but they took no heed until they felt the bullets spattering them from one side.

"Goddamn their souls, they've branded me!" Demetrio cried, his teeth flashing.

Then, very swiftly, he slid down a gully and was lost. . . .

Chapter 4

Two men were missing, Serapio the candymaker, and Antonio, who played the cymbals in the Juchipila band.

"Maybe they'll join us further on," said Demetrio.

The return journey proved moody. Anastasio Montáñez alone preserved his equanimity, a kindly expression playing in his sleepy eyes and on his bearded face. Pancracio's harsh, gorillalike profile retained its repulsive immutability.

The soldiers had retreated; Demetrio began the search for the soldiers' horses which had been hidden in the sierra.

Suddenly Quail, who had been walking ahead, shrieked. He had caught sight of his companions swinging from the branches of a mesquite. There could be no doubt of their identity; Serapio and Antonio they certainly were. Anastasio Montáñez prayed brokenly.

"Our Father Who art in heaven, hallowed be Thy name. Thy kingdom come . . ."

"Amen," his men answered in low tones, their heads bowed, their hats upon their breasts. . . .

Then, hurriedly, they took the Juchipila canyon northward, without halting to rest until nightfall.

Quail kept walking close to Anastasio, unable to banish from his mind the two who were hanged, their dislocated limp necks, their dangling legs, their arms pendulous, and their bodies moving slowly in the wind.

On the morrow, Demetrio complained bitterly of his wound; he could no longer ride on horseback. They were forced to carry him the rest of the way on a makeshift stretcher of leaves and branches.

"He's bleeding frightfully," said Anastasio Montáñez, tearing off one of his shirt-sleeves and tying it tightly about Demetrio's thigh, a little above the wound.

"That's good," said Venancio. "It'll keep him from bleeding and stop the pain."

Venancio was a barber. In his native town, he pulled teeth and fulfilled the office of medicine man. He was accorded an unimpeachable authority because he had read *The Wandering Jew* and one or two other books. They called him "Doctor"; and since he was conceited about his knowledge, he employed very few words.

They took turns, carrying the stretcher in relays of four over the bare stony mesa and up the steep passes.

At high noon, when the reflection of the sun on the calcareous soil burned their shoulders and made the landscape dimly waver before their eyes, the monotonous, rhythmical moan of the wounded rose in unison with the ceaseless cry of the locusts. They stopped to rest at every small hut they found hidden between the steep, jagged rocks.

"Thank God, a kind soul and tortillas full of beans and chili are never lacking," Anastasio Montáñez said with a triumphant belch.

The mountaineers would shake calloused hands with the travelers, saying:

"God's blessing on you! He will find a way to help you all, never fear. We're going ourselves, starting tomorrow morning. We're dodging the draft, with those damned Government people who've declared war to the death on us, on all the poor. They come and steal our pigs, our chickens and corn, they burn our homes and carry our women off, and if they ever get hold of us they'll kill us like mad dogs, and we die right there on the spot and that's the end of the story!"

At sunset, amid the flames dyeing the sky with vivid, variegated colors, they descried a group of houses up in the heart of the blue mountains. Demetrio ordered them to carry him there.

These proved to be a few wretched straw huts, dispersed all over the river slopes, between rows of young sprouting corn and beans. They lowered the stretcher and Demetrio, in a weak voice, asked for a glass of water.

Groups of squalid Indians sat in the dark pits of the huts, men with bony chests, disheveled, matted hair, and ruddy cheeks; behind them, eyes shone up from floors of fresh reeds.

A child with a large belly and glossy dark skin came close to the stretcher to inspect the wounded man. An old woman followed, and soon all of them drew about Demetrio in a circle.

A girl sympathizing with him in his plight brought a *jícara* of bluish water. With hands shaking, Demetrio took it up and drank greedily.

"Will you have some more?"

He raised his eyes and glanced at the girl, whose features were common but whose voice had a note of kindness in it. Wiping his sweating brow with the back of his palm and turning on one side, he gasped:

"May God reward you."

Then his whole body shook, making the leaves of the stretcher rustle. Fever possessed him; he fainted.

"It's a damp night and that's terrible for the fever," said Remigia, an old wrinkled barefooted woman, wearing a cloth rag for a blouse.

She invited them to move Demetrio into her hut.

Pancracio, Anastasio Montáñez, and Quail lay down beside the stretcher like faithful dogs, watchful of their master's wishes. The rest scattered about in search of food.

Remigia offered them all she had, chili and tortillas.

"Imagine! I had eggs, chickens, even a goat and her kid, but those damn soldiers wiped me out clean."

Then, making a trumpet of her hands, she drew near Anastasio and murmured in his ear:

"Imagine, they even carried away Señora Nieves' little girl!"

Chapter 5

Suddenly awakening, Quail opened his eyes and stood up.

"Montáñez, did you hear? A shot, Montáñez! Hey, Montáñez, get up!"

He shook him vigorously until Montáñez ceased snoring and in turn woke up.

"What in the name of . . . Now you're at it again, damn it. I tell you there aren't ghosts any more," Anastasio muttered out of a half-sleep.

"I heard a shot, Montáñez!"

"Go back to sleep, Quail, or I'll bust your nose."

"Hell, Anastasio, I tell you it's no nightmare. I've forgotten those fellows they hung, honest. It's a shot, I tell you. I heard it all right."

"A shot, you say? All right, then, hand me my gun."

Anastasio Montáñez rubbed his eyes, stretched out his arms and legs, and stood up lazily.

They left the hut. The sky was solid with stars; the moon rose like a sharp scythe. The confused rumor of women crying in fright resounded from the various huts; the men who had been sleeping in the open, also woke up and the rattle of arms echoed over the mountain.

"You cursed fool, you've maimed me for life."

A voice rang clearly through the darkness.

"Who goes there?"

The shout echoed from rock to rock, through mound and over hollow, until it spent itself at the far, silent reaches of the night.

"Who goes there?" Anastasio repeated his challenge lounder, pulling back the lock of his Mauser.

"One of Demetrio's men," came the answer.

"It's Pancracio," Quail cried joyfully. Relieved, he rested the butt of his rifle on the ground.

Pancracio appeared, holding a young man by the arms; the newcomer was covered with dust from his felt hat to his coarse shoes. A fresh bloodstain lay on his trousers close to the heel.

"Who's this tenderfoot?" Anastasio demanded.

"You know I'm on guard around here. Well, I hears a noise in the brush, see, and I shouts, 'Who goes there?' and then this lad answers, 'Carranza! Carranza!' I don't know anyone by that name, and so I says, 'Carranza, hell!' and I just pumps a bit of lead into his hoof."

Smiling, Pancracio turned his beardless head around as if soliciting applause.

Then the stranger spoke:

"Who's your commander?"

Proudly, Anastasio raised his head, went up to him and looked him in the face. The stranger lowered his tone considerably.

"Well, I'm a revolutionist, too, you know. The Government drafted me and I served as a private, but I managed to desert during the battle the day before yesterday, and I've been walking about in search of you all."

"So he's a Government soldier, eh?" A murmur of incredulity rose from the men, interrupting the stranger.

"So that's what you are, eh? One of those damn half-breeds," said Anastasio Montáñez. "Why the hell didn't you pump your lead in his brain, Pancracio?"

"What's he talking about, anyhow? I can't make head nor tail of it. He says he wants to see Demetrio and that he's got plenty to say to him. But that's all right: we've got plenty of time to do anything we damn well please so long as you're in no hurry, that's all," said Pancracio, loading his gun.

"What kind of beasts are you?" the prisoner cried. He could say no more: Anastasio's fist, crashing down upon his face, sent his head turning on his neck, covered with blood.

"Shoot the half-breed!"

"Hang him!"

"Burn him alive; he's a lousy Federal."

In great excitement, they yelled and shrieked and were about to fire at the prisoner.

"Sssh! Shut up! I think Demetrio's talking now," Anastasio said, striving to quiet them. Indeed, Demetrio, having ascertained the cause of the turmoil, ordered them to bring the prisoner before him.

"It's positively infamous, señor; look," Luis Cervantes said, pointing to the bloodstains on his trousers and to his bleeding face.

"All right, all right. But who in hell are you? That's what I want to know," Demetrio said.

"My name is Luis Cervantes, sir. I'm a medical student and a journalist. I wrote a piece in favor of the revolution, you see; as a result, they persecuted me, caught me, and finally landed me in the barracks."

His ensuing narrative was couched in terms of such detail and expressed in terms so melodramatic that it drew guffaws of mirth from Pancracio and Manteca.

"All I've tried to do is to make myself clear on this point. I want you to be convinced that I am truly one of your coreligionists. . . ."

"What's that? What did you say? Car . . . what?" Demetrio asked, bringing his ear close to Cervantes.

"Coreligionist, sir, that is to say, a person who possesses the same religion, who is inspired by the same ideals, who defends and fights for the same cause you are now fighting for."

Demetrio smiled:

"What *are* we fighting for? That's what I'd like to know."

In his disconcertment, Luis Cervantes could find no reply.

"Look at that mug, look at 'im! Why waste any time, Demetrio? Let's shoot him," Pancracio urged impatiently.

Demetrio laid a hand on his hair which covered his ears, and stretching himself out for a long time, seemed to be lost in thought. Having found no solution, he said:

"Get out, all of you; it's aching again. Anastasio, put out the candle. Lock him up in the corral and let Pancracio and Manteca watch him. Tomorrow, we'll see. . . ."

Chapter 6

Through the shadows of the starry night, Luis Cervantes had not yet managed to detect the exact shape of the objects about him. Seeking the most suitable resting-place, he laid his weary bones down on a fresh pile of manure under the blurred mass of a *huizache* tree. He lay down, more exhausted than resigned, and closed his eyes, resolutely determined to sleep until his fierce keepers or the morning sun, burning his ears, awakened him. Something vaguely like warmth at his side, then a tired hoarse breath, made him shudder. He opened his eyes and feeling about him with his hands, he sensed the coarse hairs of a large pig which, resenting the presence of a neighbor, began to grunt.

All Luis' efforts to sleep proved quite useless, not only because the pain of his wound or the bruises on his flesh smarted, but because he suddenly realized the exact nature of his failure.

Yes, failure! For he had never learned to appreciate exactly the difference between fulminating sentences of death upon bandits in the columns of a small country newspaper and actually setting out in search of them, and tracking them to their lairs, gun in hand. During his first day's march as volunteer lieutenant, he had begun to suspect the error of his ways—a brutal sixty miles' journey it was, that left his hips and legs one mass of raw soreness and soldered all his bones together. A week later, after his first skirmish against the rebels, he understood every rule of the game. Luis Cervantes would have taken up a crucifix and solemnly sworn that as soon as the soldiers, gun in hand, stood ready to shoot, some profoundly eloquent voice had spoken behind them, saying, "Run for your lives." It was all crystal clear. Even his noble-spirited horse, accustomed to battle, sought to sweep back on its hind legs and gallop furiously away, to stop only at a safe distance from the sound of firing. The sun was setting, the mountain became peopled with vague and restless shadows, darkness scaled the ramparts of the mountain hastily. What could be more logical then, than to seek refuge behind the rocks and attempt to sleep, granting mind and body a sorely needed rest?

But the soldier's logic is the logic of absurdity. On the morrow, for example, his colonel awakened him rudely out of his sleep, cuffing and belaboring him unmercifully, and, after having bashed in his face, deprived him of his place of vantage. The rest of the officers, moreover, burst into hilarious mirth and holding their sides with laughter begged the colonel to pardon the deserter. The colonel, therefore, instead of sentencing him to be shot, kicked his buttocks roundly for him and assigned him to kitchen police.

This signal insult was destined to bear poisonous fruit. Luis Cervantes determined to play turncoat; indeed, mentally, he had already changed sides. Did not the sufferings of the underdogs, of the disinherited masses, move him to the core? Henceforth he espoused the cause of Demos, of the subjugated, the beaten and baffled, who implore justice, and justice alone. He became intimate with the humblest private. More, even, he shed tears of compassion over a dead mule which fell, load and all, after a terribly long journey.

From then on, Luis Cervantes' prestige with the soldiers increased. Some actually dared to make confessions. One among them, conspicuous for his sobriety and silence, told him: "I'm a carpenter by trade, you know. I had a mother, an old woman nailed to her chair for ten years by rheumatism. In the middle of the night, they pulled me out of my house; three damn policemen; I woke up a soldier twenty-five miles away from my hometown. A month ago our company passed by there again. My mother was already under the sod! . . . So there's nothing left for me in this wide world; no one misses me now, you see. But, by God, I'm damned if I'll use these cartridges they make us carry, against the enemy. If a miracle happens (I pray for it every night, you know, and I guess our Lady of Guadalupe can do it all right), then I'll join Villa's men; and I swear by the holy soul of my old mother, that I'll make every one of these Government people pay, by God I will."

Another soldier, a bright young fellow, but a charlatan at heart, who drank habitually and smoked the narcotic marihuana weed, eyeing him with vague, glassy stare, whispered in his ear, "You know, partner . . . the men on the other side . . . you know, the other side . . . you understand. . .they ride the best horses up north there, and all over, see? And they harness their mounts with pure hammered silver. But us? Oh hell, we've got to ride plugs, that's all, and not one of them good enough to stagger round a water well. You see, don't you, partner? You see what I mean? You know, the men on the other side—they get shiny new silver coins while we get only lousy paper money printed in that murderer's factory, that's what we get, yes, that's ours, I tell you!"

The majority of the soldiers spoke in much the same tenor. Even a top sergeant candidly confessed, "Yes, I enlisted all right. I wanted to. But, by God, I missed the right side by a long shot. What you can't make in a lifetime, sweating like a mule and breaking your back in peacetime, damn it all, you can make in a few months just running around the sierra with a gun on your back, but not with this crowd, dearie, not with this lousy outfit. . . ."

Luis Cervantes, who already shared this hidden, implacably mortal hatred of the upper classes, of his officers, and of his superiors, felt that a veil had been removed from his eyes; clearly, now, he saw the final outcome of the struggle. And yet what had happened? The first moment he was able to join his coreligionists, instead of welcoming him with open arms, they threw him into a pigsty with swine for company.

Day broke. The roosters crowed in the huts. The chickens perched in the *huizache* began to stretch their wings, shake their feathers, and fly down to the ground.

Luis Cervantes saw his guards lying on top of a dung heap, snoring. In his imagination, he reviewed the features of last night's men. One, Pancracio, was pock-marked, blotchy, unshaven; his chin protruded, his forehead receded obliquely; his ears formed one solid piece with head and neck—a horrible man. The other, Manteca, was so much human refuse; his eyes were almost hidden, his look sullen; his wiry straight hair fell over his ears, forehead and neck; his scrofulous lips hung eternally agape. Once more, Luis Cervantes felt his flesh quiver.

Chapter 7

Still drowsy, Demetrio ran his hand through his ruffled hair, which hung over his moist forehead, pushed it back over his ears, and opened his eyes.

Distinctly he heard the woman's melodious voice which he had already sensed in his dream. He walked toward the door.

It was broad daylight; the rays of sunlight filtered through the thatch of the hut.

The girl who had offered him water the day before, the girl of whom he had dreamed all night long, now came forward, kindly and eager as ever. This time she carried a pitcher of milk brimming over with foam.

"It's goat's milk, but fine just the same. Come on now: taste it."

Demetrio smiled gratefully, straightened up, grasped the clay pitcher, and proceeded to drink the milk in little gulps, without removing his eyes from the girl.

She grew self-conscious, lowered her eyes.

"What's your name?" he asked.

"Camilla."

"Ah, there's a lovely name! And the girl that bears it, lovelier still!"

Camilla blushed. As he sought to seize her wrist, she grew frightened, and picking up the empty pitcher, flew out the door.

"No, Demetrio," Anastasio Montáñez commented gravely, "you've got to break them in first. Hmm! It's a hell of a lot of scars the women have left on my body. Yes, my friend, I've a heap of experience along that line."

"I feel all right now, Compadre." Demetrio pretended he had not heard him. "I had fever, and I sweated like a horse all night, but I feel quite fresh today. The thing that's irking me hellishly is that Goddamn wound. Call Venancio to look after me."

"What are we going to do with the tenderfoot we caught last night?" Pancracio asked.

"That's right: I was forgetting all about him."

As usual, Demetrio hesitated a while before he reached a decision.

"Here, Quail, come here. Listen: you go and find out where's the nearest church around here. I know there's one about six miles away. Go and steal a priest's robe and bring it back."

"What's the idea?" asked Pancracio in surprise.

"Well, I'll soon find out if this tenderfoot came here to murder me. I'll tell him he's to be shot, see, and Quail will put on the priest's robes, say that he's a priest and hear his confession. If he's got anything up his sleeve, he'll come out with it, and then I'll shoot him. Otherwise I'll let him go."

"God, there's a roundabout way to tackle the question. If I were you, I'd just shoot him and let it go at that," said Pancracio contemptuously.

That night Quail returned with the priest's robes; Demetrio ordered the prisoner to be led in. Luis Cervantes had not eaten or slept for two days, there were deep black circles under his eyes; his face was deathly pale, his lips dry and colorless. He spoke awkwardly, slowly: "You can do as you please with me. . . . I am convinced I was wrong to looking for you."

There was a prolonged silence. Then:

"I thought that you would welcome a man who comes to offer his help, with open arms, even though his help was quite worthless. After all, you might perhaps have found some use for it. What, in heaven's name, do I stand to gain, whether the revolution wins or loses?"

Little by little he grew more animated; at times the languor in his eyes disappeared.

"The revolution benefits the poor, the ignorant, all those who have been slaves all their lives, all the unhappy people who do not even suspect they are poor because the rich who stand above them, the rich who rule them, change their sweat and blood and tears into gold. . . ."

"Well, what the hell is the gist of all this palaver? I'll be damned if I can stomach a sermon," Pancracio broke in.

"I wanted to fight for the sacred cause of the oppressed, but you don't understand . . . you cast me aside. . . . Very well, then, you can do as you please with me!"

"All I'm going to do now is to put this rope around your neck. Look what a pretty white neck you've got."

"Yes, I know what brought you here," Demetrio interrupted dryly, scratching his head. "I'm going to have you shot!"

Then, looking at Anastasio, he said:

"Take him away. And . . . if he wants to confess, bring the priest to him."

Impassive as ever, Anastasio took the prisoner gently by the arm.

"Come along this way, Tenderfoot."

They all laughed uproariously, when a few minutes later, Quail appeared in priestly robes.

"By God, this tenderfoot certainly talks his head off," Quail said. "You know, I've a notion he was having a bit of a laugh on me when I started asking him questions."

"But didn't he have anything to say?"

"Nothing, save what he said last night."

"I've a hunch he didn't come here to shoot you at all, Compadre," said Anastasio.

"Give him something to eat and guard him."

Chapter 8

On the morrow, Luis Cervantes was barely able to get up. His injured leg trailing behind him, he shuffled from hut to hut in search of a little alcohol, a kettle of boiled water and some rags. With unfailing kindness, Camilla provided him with all that he wanted.

As he began washing his foot, she sat beside him, and, with typical mountaineer's curiosity, inquired:

"Tell me, who learned you how to cure people? Why did you boil that water? Why did you boil the rags? Look, look, how careful you are about everything! And what did you put on your hands? Really. . . . And why did you pour on alcohol? I just knew alcohol was good to rub on when you had a bellyache, but . . . Oh, I see! So you was going to be a doctor, huh? Ha, ha, that's a good one! Why don't you mix it with cold water! Well, there's a funny sort of a trick. Oh, stop fooling me . . . the idea: little animals alive in the water unless you boil it! Ugh! Well, I can't see nothing in it myself."

Camilla continued to cross-question him with such familiarity that she suddenly found herself addressing him intimately, in the singular *tu*. Absorbed in his own thoughts, Luis Cervantes had ceased listening to her. He thought:

Where are those men on Pancho Villa's payroll, so admirably equipped and mounted, who only get paid in those pure silver pieces Villa coins at the Chihuahua mint? Bah! Barely two dozen half-naked mangy men, some of them riding decrepit mares with the coat nibbled off from neck to withers. Can the accounts given by the Government newspapers and by myself be really true and are these so-called revolutionists simply bandits grouped together, using the revolution as a wonderful pretext to glut their thirst for gold and blood? Is it all a lie, then? Were their sympathizers talking a lot of exalted nonsense?

If on one hand the Government newspapers vied with each other in noisy proclamation of Federal victory after victory, why then had a paymaster on his way from Guadalajara started the rumor that President Huerta's friends and relatives were abandoning the capital and scurrying away to the nearest port? Was Huerta's, "I shall have peace, at no matter what cost," a meaningless growl? Well, it looked as though the revolutionists or bandits, call them what you will, were going to depose the Government. Tomorrow would therefore belong wholly to them. A man must consequently be on their side, only on their side.

"No," he said to himself almost aloud, "I don't think I've made a mistake this time."

"What did you say?" Camilla asked. "I thought you'd lost your tongue. . . . I thought the mice had eaten it up!"

Luis Cervantes frowned and cast a hostile glance at this little plump monkey with her bronzed complexion, her ivory teeth, and her thick square toes.

"Look here, Tenderfoot, you know how to tell fairy stories, don't you?"

For all answer, Luis made an impatient gesture and moved off, the girl's ecstatic glance following his retreating figure until it was lost on the river path. So profound was her absorption that she shuddered in nervous surprise as she heard the voice of her neighbor, one-eyed María Antonia, who had been spying from her hut, shouting:

"Hey, you there: give him some love powder. Then he might fall for you."

"That's what you'd do, all right!"

"Oh, you think so, do you? Well, you're quite wrong! Faugh! I despise a tenderfoot, and don't forget it!"

Chapter 9

"Ho there, Remigia, lend me some eggs, will you? My chicken has been hatching since morning. There's some gentlemen here, come to eat."

Her neighbor's eyes blinked as the bright sunlight poured into the shadowy hut, darker than usual, even, as dense clouds of smoke rose from the stove. After a few minutes, she began to make out the contour of the various objects inside, and recognized the wounded man's stretcher, which lay in one corner, close to the ashy-gray galvanized iron roof.

She sat down beside Remigia Indian-fashion, and, glancing furtively toward where Demetrio rested, asked in a low voice:

"How's the patient, better? That's fine. Oh, how young he is! But he's still pale, don't you think? So the wound's not closed up yet. Well, Remigia, don't you think we'd better try and do something about it?"

Remigia, naked from the waist up, stretched her thin muscular arms over the corn grinder, pounding the corn with a stone bar she held in her hands.

"Oh, I don't know; they might not like it," she answered, breathing heavily as she continued her rude task. "They've got their own doctor, you know, so—"

"Hallo, there, Remigia," another neighbor said as she came in, bowing her bony back to pass through the opening, "haven't you any laurel leaves? We want to make a potion for María Antonia who's not so well today, what with her bellyache."

In reality, her errand was but a pretext for asking questions and passing the time of day in gossip, so she turned her eyes to the corner where the patient lay and, winking, sought information as to his health.

Remigia lowered her eyes to indicate that Demetrio was sleeping.

"Oh, I didn't see you when I came in. And you're here too, Panchita? Well, how are you?"

"Good morning to you, Fortunata. How are you?"

"All right. But María Antonia's got the curse today and her belly's aching something fierce."

She sat Indian-fashion, with bent knees, huddling hip to hip against Panchita.

"I've got no laurel leaves, honey," Remigia answered, pausing a moment in her work to push a mop of hair back from over her sweaty forehead. Then, plunging her two hands into a mass of corn, she removed a handful of it dripping with muddy yellowish water. "I've none at all; you'd better go to Dolores, she's always got herbs, you know."

"But Dolores went to Cofradía last night. I don't know, but they say they came to fetch her to help Uncle Matías' girl who's big with child."

"You don't say, Panchita?"

The three old women came together forming an animated group, and speaking in low tones, began to gossip with great gusto.

"Certainly, I swear it, by God up there in heaven."

"Well, well, I was the first one to say that Marcelina was big with child, wasn't I? But of course no one would believe me."

"Poor girl. It's going to be terrible if the kid is her uncle's, you know!"

"God forbid!"

"Of course it's not her uncle: Nazario had nothing to do with it, I know. It was them damned soldiers, that's who done it."

"God, what a bloody mess! Another unhappy woman!"

The cackle of the old hens finally awakened Demetrio. They kept silent for a moment; then Panchita, taking out of the bosom of her blouse a young pigeon which opened its beak in suffocation, said:

"To tell you the truth, I brought this medicine for the gentleman here, but they say he's got a doctor, so I suppose—"

"That makes no difference, Panchita, that's no medicine anyhow, it's simply something to rub on his body."

"Forgive this poor gift from a poor woman, señor," said the wrinkled old woman, drawing close to Demetrio, "but there's nothing like it in the world for hemorrhages and suchlike."

Demetrio nodded hasty approval. They had already placed a loaf of bread soaked in alcohol on his stomach; although when this was removed he began to be cooler, he felt that he was still feverish inside.

"Come on, Remigia, you do it, you certainly know how," the women said.

Out of a reed sheath, Remigia pulled a long and curved knife which served to cut cactus fruit. She took the pigeon in one hand, turned it over, its breast upward, and with the skill of a surgeon, ripped it in two with a single thrust.

"In the name of Jesus, Mary, and Joseph," Remigia said, blessing the room and making the sign of the cross; next, with infinite dexterity, she placed the warm bleeding portions of the pigeon upon Demetrio's abdomen.

"You'll see: you'll feel much better now."

Obeying Remigia's instructions, Demetrio lay motionless, crumpled up on one side.

Then Fortunata gave vent to her sorrows. She liked these gentlemen of the revolution, all right, that she did—for, three months ago, you know, the Government soldiers had run away with her only daughter. This had broken her heart, yes, and driven her all but crazy.

As she began, Anastasio Montáñez and Quail lay on the floor near the stretcher, their mouths gaping, all ears to the story. But Fortunata's wealth of detail by the time she had told half of it bored Quail and he left the hut to scratch himself out in the sun. By the time Fortunata had at last concluded with a solemn "I pray God and the Blessed Virgin Mary that you are not sparing the life of a single one of those Federals from hell," Demetrio, face to wall, felt greatly relieved by the stomach cure, and was busy thinking of the best route by which to proceed to Durango. Anastasio Montáñez was snoring like a trombone.

Chapter 10

"Why don't you call in the tenderfoot to treat you, Compadre Demetrio," Anastasio Montáñez asked his chief, who had been complaining daily of chills and fever. "You ought to see him; no one has laid a hand to him but himself, and now he's so fit that he doesn't limp a step."

But Venancio, standing by with his tins of lard and his dirty string rags ready, protested:

"All right, if anybody lays a hand on Demetrio, I won't be responsible."

"Nonsense! Rot! What kind of doctor do you think you are? You're no doctor at all. I'll wager you've already forgotten why you ever joined us," said Quail.

"Well, I remember why you joined us, Quail," Venancio replied angrily. "Perhaps you'll deny it was because you had stolen a watch and some diamond rings."

"Ha, ha, ha! That's rich! But you're worse, my lad; you ran away from your hometown because you poisoned your sweetheart."

"You're a Goddamned liar!"

"Yes you did! And don't try and deny it! You fed her Spanish fly and . . ."

Venancio's shout of protest was drowned out in the loud laughter of the others. Demetrio, looking pale and sallow, motioned for silence. Then, plaintively:

"That'll do. Bring in the student."

Luis Cervantes entered. He uncovered Demetrio's wound, examined it carefully, and shook his head. The ligaments had made a furrow in the skin. The leg, badly swollen, seemed about to burst. At every move he made, Demetrio stifled a moan. Luis Cervantes cut the ligaments, soaked the wound in water, covered the leg with large clean rags and bound it up. Demetrio was able to sleep all afternoon and all night. On the morrow he woke up happy.

"That tenderfoot has the softest hand in the world!" he said.

Quickly Venancio cut in:

"All right; just as you say. But don't forget that tenderfoots are like moisture, they seep in everywhere. It's the tenderfoots who stopped us reaping the harvest of the revolution."

Since Demetrio believed in the barber's knowledge implicitly, when Luis Cervantes came to treat him on the next day he said:

"Look here, do your best, see. I want to recover soon and then you can go home or anywhere else you damn well please."

Discreetly, Luis Cervantes made no reply.

A week, ten days, a fortnight elapsed. The Federal troops seemed to have vanished. There was an abundance of corn and beans, too, in the neighboring ranches. The people hated the Government so bitterly that they were overjoyed to furnish assistance to the rebels. Demetrio's men, therefore, were peacefully waiting for the complete recovery of their chief.

Day after day, Luis Cervantes remained humble and silent.

"By God, I actually believe you're in love," Demetrio said jokingly one morning after the daily treatment. He had begun to like this tenderfoot. From then on, Demetrio began gradually to show an increasing interest in Cervantes' comfort. One day he asked him if the soldiers gave him his daily ration of meat and milk; Luis Cervantes was forced to answer that his sole nourishment was whatever the old ranch women happened to give him and that everyone still considered him an intruder.

"Look here, Tenderfoot, they're all good boys, really," Demetrio answered. "You've got to know how to handle them, that's all. You mark my words; from tomorrow on, there won't be a thing you'll lack."

In effect, things began to change that very afternoon. Some of Demetrio's men lay in the quarry, glancing at the sunset that turned the clouds into huge clots of congealed blood and listening to Venancio's amusing stories culled from *The Wandering Jew*. Some of them, lulled by the narrator's mellifluous voice, began to snore. But Luis Cervantes listened avidly and as soon as Venancio topped off his talk with a storm of anticlerical denunciations he said emphatically: "Wonderful, wonderful! What intelligence! You're a most gifted man!"

"Well, I reckon it's not so bad," Venancio answered, warming to the flattery, "but my parents died and I didn't have a chance to study for a profession."

"That's easy to remedy, I'm sure. Once our cause is victorious, you can easily get a degree. A matter of two or three weeks' assistant's work at some hospital and a letter of recommendation from our chief and you'll be a full-fledged doctor, all right. The thing is child's play."

From that night onward Venancio, unlike the others, ceased calling him Tenderfoot. He addressed him as Louie.

It was Louie, this, and Louie, that, right and left, all the time.

Chapter 11

"Look here, Tenderfoot, I want to tell you something," Camilla called to Luis Cervantes, as he made his way to the hut to fetch some boiling water for his foot.

For days the girl had been restless. Her coy ways and her reticence had finally annoyed the man; stopping suddenly, he stood up and eyeing her squarely:

"All right. What do you want to tell me?"

Camilla's tongue clove to her mouth, heavy and damp as a rag; she could not utter a word. A blush suffused her cheeks, turning them red as apples; she shrugged her shoulders and bowed her head, pressing her chin against her naked breast. Then without moving, with the fixity of an idiot, she glanced at the wound, and said in a whisper:

"Look, how nicely it's healing now: it's like a red Castille rose."

Luis Cervantes frowned and with obvious disgust continued to care for his foot, completely ignoring her as he worked. When he had finished, Camilla had vanished.

For three days she was nowhere to be found. It was always her mother, Agapita, who answered Cervantes' call, and boiled the water for him and gave him rags. He was careful to avoid questioning her. Three days later, Camilla reappeared, more coy and eager than ever.

The more distrait and indifferent Luis Cervantes grew, the bolder Camilla. At last, she said: "Listen to me, you nice young fellow, I want to tell you something pleasant. Please go over the words of the revolutionary song 'Adelita' with me, will you? You can guess why, eh? I want to sing it and sing it, over again often and often, see? Then when you're off and away and when you've forgotten all about Camilla, it'll remind me of you."

To Luis Cervantes her words were like the noise of a sharp steel knife drawn over the side of a glass bottle. Blissfully unaware of the effect they had produced, she proceeded, candid as ever:

"Well, I want to tell you something. You don't know that your chief is a wicked man, do you? Shall I tell you what he did to me? You know Demetrio won't let a soul but Mamma cook for him and me take him his food. Well, the other day I take some food over to him and what do you think he did to me, the old fool. He grabs hold of my wrist and he presses it tight, tight as can be, and then he starts pinching my legs.

"'Come on, let me go,' I said. 'Keep still, lay off, you shameless creature. You've got no manners, that's the trouble with you.' So I wrestled with him, and shook myself free, like this, and ran off as fast as I could. What do you think of that?"

Camilla had never seen Luis Cervantes laugh so heartily.

"But it is really true, all this you've told me?"

Utterly at a loss, Camilla could not answer. Then he burst into laughter again and repeated the question. A sense of confusion came upon her. Disturbed, troubled, she said brokenly:

"Yes, it's the truth. And I wanted to tell you about it. But you don't seem to feel at all angry."

Once more Camilla glanced adoringly at Luis Cervantes' radiant, clean face; at his glaucous, soft eyes, his cheeks pink and polished as a porcelain doll's; at his tender white skin that showed below the line of his collar and on his shoulders, protruding from under a rough woolen poncho; at his hair, ever so slightly curled.

"What the devil are you waiting for, fool? If the

chief likes you, what more do you want?"

Camilla felt something rise within her breast, an empty ache that became a knot when it reached her throat; she closed her eyes fast to hold back the tears that welled up in them. Then, with the back of her hand, she wiped her wet cheeks, and just as she had done three days ago, fled with all the swiftness of a young deer.

Chapter 12

Demetrio's wound had already healed. They began to discuss various projects to go northward where, according to rumor, the rebels had beaten the Federal troops all along the line.

A certain incident came to precipitate their action. Seated on a crag of the sierra in the cool of the afternoon breeze, Luis Cervantes gazed away in the distance, dreaming and killing time. Below the narrow rock Pancracio and Manteca, lying like lizards between the *jarales* along one of the river margins, were playing cards. Anastasio Montáñez, looking on indifferently, turned his black hairy face toward Luis Cervantes and, leveling his kindly gaze upon him, asked:

"Why so sad, you from the city? What are you daydreaming about? Come on over here and let's have a chat!"

Luis Cervantes did not move; Anastasio went over to him and sat down beside him like a friend.

"What you need is the excitement of the city. I wager you shine your shoes every day and wear a necktie. Now, I may look dirty and my clothes may be torn to shreds, but I'm not really what I seem to be. I'm not here because I've got to be and don't you think so. Why, I own twenty oxen. Certainly I do; ask my friend Demetrio. I cleared ten bushels last harvest time. You see, if there's one thing I love, that's riling these Government fellows and making them furious. The last scrape I had—it'll be eight months gone now, ever since I've joined these men—I stuck my knife into some captain. He was just a nobody, a little Government squirt. I pinked him here, see, right under the navel. And that's why I'm here: that and because I wanted to give my mate Demetrio a hand."

"Christ! The bloody little darling of my life!" Manteca shouted, waxing enthusiastic over a winning hand. He placed a twenty-cent silver coin on the jack of spades.

"If you want my opinion, I'm not much on gambling. Do you want to bet? Well, come on then, I'm game. How do you like the sound of this leather snake jingling, eh?"

Anastasio shook his belt; the silver coins rang as he shook them together.

Meanwhile, Pancracio dealt the cards, the jack of spades turned up out of the deck and a quarrel ensued. Altercation, noise, then shouts, and, at last, insults. Pancracio brought his stony face close to Manteca, who looked at him with snake's eyes, convulsive, foaming at the mouth. Another moment and they would have been exchanging blows. Having completely exhausted their stock of direct insults, they now resorted to the most flowery and ornate insulting of each other's ancestors, male and female, paternal or maternal. Yet nothing untoward occurred.

After their supply of words was exhausted, they gave over gambling and, their arms about each other's shoulders, marched off in search of a drink of alcohol.

"I don't like to fight with my tongue either, it's not decent. I'm right, too, eh? I tell you no man living has ever breathed a word to me against my mother. I want to be respected, see? That's why you've never seen me fooling with anyone." There was a pause. Then, suddenly, "Look there, Tenderfoot," Anastasio said, changing his tone and standing up with one hand spread over his eyes. "What's that dust over there behind the hillock. By God, what if it's those damned Federals and we sitting here doing nothing. Come on, let's go and warn the rest of the boys."

The news met with cries of joy.

"Ah, we're going to meet them!" cried Pancracio jubilantly, first among them to rejoice.

"Of course, we're going to meet them! We'll strip them clean of everything they brought with them."

A few moments later, amid cries of joy and a bustle of arms, they began saddling their horses. But the enemy turned out to be a few burros and two Indians, driving them forward.

"Stop them, anyhow. They must have come from somewhere and they've probably news for us," Demetrio said.

Indeed, their news proved sensational. The Federal troops had fortified the hills in Zacatecas; this was said to be Huerta's last stronghold, but everybody predicted the fall of the city. Many families had hastily fled southward. Trains were overloaded with people; there was a scarcity of trucks and coaches; hundreds of people, panic-stricken, walked along the highroad with their belongings in a pack slung over their shoulders. General Pánfilo Natera was assembling his men at Fresnillo; the Federals already felt it was all up with them.

"The fall of Zacatecas will be Huerta's *requiescat in pace*," Luis Cervantes cried with unusual excitement. "We've got to be there before the fight starts so that we can join Natera's army."

Then, suddenly, he noted the surprise with which Demetrio and his men greeted his suggestion. Crestfallen, he realized they still considered him of no account.

On the morrow, as the men set off in search of good mounts before taking to the road again, Demetrio called Luis Cervantes:

"Do you really want to come with us? Of course you're cut from another timber, we all know that; God knows why you should like this sort of life. Do you imagine we're in this game because we like it? Now, I like the excitement all right, but that's not all. Sit down here; that's right. Do you want to know why I'm a rebel? Well, I'll tell you.

"Before the revolution, I had my land all plowed, see, and just right for sowing and if it hadn't been for a little quarrel with Don Mónico, the boss of my town, Moyahua, I'd be there in a jiffy getting the oxen ready for the sowing, see?

"Here, there, Pancracio, pull down two bottles of beer for me and this tenderfoot. . . . By the Holy Cross . . . drinking won't hurt me, now, will it?"

Chapter 13

"I was born in Limón, close by Moyahua, right in the heart of the Juchipila canyon. I had my house and my cows and a patch of land, see: I had everything I wanted. Well, I suppose you know how we farmers make a habit of going over to town every week to hear Mass and the sermon and then to market to buy our onions and tomatoes and in general everything they want us to buy at the ranch. Then you pick up some friends and go to Primitivo López' saloon for a bit of a drink before dinner; well, you sit there drinking and you've got to be sociable, so you drink more than you should and the liquor goes to your head and you laugh and you're damned happy and if you feel like it, you sing and shout and kick up a bit of a row. That's quite all right, anyhow, for we're not doing anyone any harm. But soon they start bothering you and the policeman walks up and down and stops occasionally, with his ear to the door. To put it in a nutshell, the chief of police and his gang are a lot of joykillers who decide they want to put a stop to your fun, see? But by God! You've got guts, you've got red blood in your veins and you've got a soul, too, see? So you lose your temper, you stand up to them and tell them to go to the Devil.

"Now if they understand you, everything's all right; they leave you alone and that's all there is to it; but sometimes they try to talk you down and hit you and—well, you know how it is, a fellow's quick-tempered and he'll be damned if he'll stand for someone ordering him around and telling him what's what. So before you know it, you've got your knife out or your gun leveled, and then off you go for a wild run in the sierra, until they've forgotten the corpse, see?

"All right: that's just about what happened to Mónico. The fellow was a greater bluffer than the rest. He couldn't tell a rooster from a hen, not he. Well, I spit on his beard because he wouldn't mind his own business. That's all, there's nothing else to tell.

"Then, just because I did that, he had the whole Goddamned Federal Government against me. You must have heard something about that story in Mexico City—about the killing of Madero and some other fellow, Félix or Felipe Díaz, or something—I don't know. Well, this man Mónico goes in person to Zacatecas to get an army to capture me. They said that I was a Maderista and that I was going to rebel. But a man like me always has friends. Somebody came and warned me of what was coming to me, so when the soldiers reached Limón I was miles and miles away. Trust me! Then my compadre Anastasio who killed somebody came and joined me, and Pancracio and Quail and a lot of friends and acquaintances came after him. Since then we've been sort of collecting, see? You know for yourself, we get along as best we can. . . ."

For a while, both men sat meditating in silence. Then:

"Look here, Chief," said Luis Cervantes. "You know that some of Natera's men are at Juchipila, quite near here. I think we should join them before they capture Zacatecas. All we need do is speak to the General."

"I'm no good at that sort of thing. And I don't like the idea of accepting orders from anybody very much."

"But you've only a handful of men down here; you'll only be an unimportant chieftain. There's no argument about it, the revolution is bound to win. After it's all over they'll talk to you just as Madero talked to all those who had helped him: 'Thank you very much, my friends, you can go home now. . . .'"

"Well that's all I want, to be let alone so I can go home."

"Wait a moment, I haven't finished. Madero said: 'You men have made me President of the Republic. You have run the risk of losing your lives and leaving your wives and children destitute; now I have what I wanted, you can go back to your picks and shovels, you can resume your hand-to-mouth existence, you can go half-naked and hungry just as you did before, while we, your superiors, will go about trying to pile up a few million pesos. . . .'"

Demetrio nodded and, smiling, scratched his head.

"You said a mouthful, Louie," Venancio the barber put in enthusiastically. "A mouthful as big as a church!"

"As I was saying," Luis Cervantes resumed, "when the revolution is over, everything is over. Too bad that so many men have been killed, too bad there are so many widows and orphans, too bad there was so much bloodshed.

"Of course, you are not selfish; you say to yourself: 'All I want to do is go back home.' But I ask you, is it fair to deprive your wife and kids of a fortune which God himself places within reach of your hand? Is it fair to abandon your motherland in this solemn moment when she most needs the self-sacrifice of her sons, when she most needs her humble sons to save her from falling again in the clutches of her eternal oppressors, executioners, and *caciques?* You must not forget that the thing a man holds most sacred on earth is his motherland."

Macías smiled, his eyes shining.

"Will it be all right if we go with Natera?"

"Not only all right," Venancio said insinuatingly, "but I think it absolutely necessary."

"Now Chief," Cervantes pursued, "I took a fancy to you the first time I laid eyes on you and I like you more and more every day because I realize what you are worth. Please let me be utterly frank. You do not yet realize your lofty noble function. You are a modest man without ambitions, you do not wish to realize the exceedingly important role you are destined to play in the revolution. It is not true that you took up arms simply because of Señor Mónico. You are under arms to protest against the evils of all the *caciques* who are overrunning the whole nation. We are the elements of a social movement which will not rest until it has enlarged the destinies of our motherland. We are the tools Destiny makes use of to reclaim the sacred rights of the people. We are not fighting to dethrone a miserable murderer, we are fighting against tyranny itself. What moves us is what men call ideals; our action is what men call fighting for a principle. A principle! That's why Villa and Natera and Carranza are fighting; that's why we, every man of us, are fighting."

"Yes . . . yes . . . exactly what I've been thinking myself," said Venancio in a climax of enthusiasm.

"Hey, there, Pancracio," Macías called, "pull down two more beers."

Chapter 14

"You ought to see how clear that fellow can make things, Compadre," Demetrio said. All morning long he had been pondering as much of Luis Cervantes' speech as he had understood.

"I heard him too," Anastasio answered. "People who can read and write get things clear, all right; nothing was ever truer. But what I can't make out is how you're going to go and meet Natera with as few men as we have."

"That's nothing. We're going to do things different now. They tell me that as soon as Crispín Robles enters a town he gets hold of all the horses and guns in the place; then he goes to the jail and lets all the jailbirds out, and, before you know it, he's got plenty of men, all right. You'll see. You know I'm beginning to feel that we haven't done things right so far. It don't seem right somehow that this city guy should be able to tell us what to do."

"Ain't it wonderful to be able to read and write!"

They both sighed, sadly. Luis Cervantes came in with several others to find out the day of their departure.

"We're leaving no later than tomorrow," said Demetrio without hesitation.

Quail suggested that musicians be summoned from the neighboring hamlet and that a farewell dance be given. His idea met with enthusiasm on all sides.

"We'll go, then," Pancracio shouted, "but I'm certainly going in good company this time. My sweetheart's coming along with me!"

Demetrio replied that he too would willingly take along a girl he had set his eye on, but that he hoped none of his men would leave bitter memories behind them as the Federals did.

"You won't have long to wait. Everything will be arranged when you return," Luis Cervantes whispered to him.

"What do you mean?" Demetrio asked. "I thought that you and Camilla . . ."

"There's not a word of truth in it, Chief. She likes you but she's afraid of you, that's all."

"Really? Is that really true?"

"Yes. But I think you're quite right in not wanting to leave any bitter feelings behind you as you go. When you come back as a conqueror, everything will be different. They'll all thank you for it even."

"By God, you're certainly a shrewd one," Demetrio replied, patting him on the back.

At sundown, Camilla went to the river to fetch water as usual. Luis Cervantes, walking down the same trail, met her. Camilla felt her heart leap to her mouth. But, without taking the slightest notice of her, Luis Cervantes hastily took one of the turns and disappeared among the rocks.

At this hour, as usual, the calcinated rocks, the sunburnt branches, and the dry weeds faded into the semiobscurity of the shadows. The wind blew softly, the green lances of the young corn leaves rustling in the twilight. Nothing was changed; all nature was as she had found it before, evening upon evening; but in the stones and the dry weeds, amid the fragrance of the air and the light whir of falling leaves, Camilla sensed a new strangeness, a vast desolation in everything about her.

Rounding a huge eroded rock, suddenly Camilla found herself face to face with Luis, who was seated on a stone, hatless, his legs dangling.

"Listen, you might come down here to say good-bye."

Luis Cervantes was obliging enough; he jumped down and joined her.

"You're proud, ain't you? Have I been so mean that you don't even want to talk to me?"

"Why do you say that, Camilla? You've been extremely kind to me; why, you've been more than a friend, you've taken care of me as if you were my sister. Now I'm about to leave, I'm very grateful to you; I'll always remember you."

"Liar!" Camilla said, her face transfigured with joy. "Suppose I hadn't come after you?"

"I intended to say good-bye to you at the dance this evening."

"What dance? If there's a dance, I'll not go to it."

"Why not?"

"Because I can't stand that horrible man . . . Demetrio!"

"Don't be silly, child," said Luis. "He's really very fond of you. Don't go and throw away this opportunity. You'll never have one like it again in your life. Don't you know that Demetrio is on the point of becoming a general, you silly girl? He'll be a very wealthy man, with horses galore; and you'll have jewels and clothes and a fine house and a lot of money to spend. Just imagine what a life you would lead with him!"

Camilla stared up at the blue sky so he should not read the expression in her eyes. A dead leaf shook slowly loose from the crest of a tree swinging slowly on the wind, fell like a small dead butterfly at her feet. She bent down and took it in her fingers. Then, without looking at him, she murmured:

"It's horrible to hear you talk like that. . . . I like you . . . no one else. . . . Ah, well, go then, go: I feel ashamed now. Please leave me!"

She threw away the leaf she had crumpled in her hand and covered her face with a corner of her apron. When she opened her eyes, Luis Cervantes had disappeared.

She followed the river trail. The river seemed to have been sprinkled with a fine red dust. On its surface drifted now a sky of variegated colors, now the dark crags, half light, half shadow. Myriads of luminous insects twinkled in a hollow. Camilla, standing on the beach of washed, round stones, caught a reflection of herself in the waters; she saw herself in her yellow blouse with the green ribbons, her white skirt, her carefully combed hair, her wide eyebrows and broad forehead, exactly as she had dressed to please Luis. She burst into tears.

Among the reeds, the frogs chanted the implacable melancholy of the hour. Perched on a dry root, a dove wept also.

Chapter 15

That evening, there was much merrymaking at the dance, and a great quantity of *mezcal* was drunk.

"I miss Camilla," said Demetrio in a loud voice.

Everybody looked about for Camilla.

"She's sick, she's got a headache," said Agapita harshly, uneasy as she caught sight of the malicious glances leveled at her.

When the dance was over, Demetrio, somewhat unsteady on his feet, thanked all the kind neighbors who had welcomed them and promised that when the revolution had triumphed he would remember them one and all, because "hospital or jail is a true test of friendship."

"May God's hand lead you all," said an old woman.

"God bless you all and keep you well," others added.

Utterly drunk, María Antonia said:

"Come back soon, damn soon!"

On the morrow, María Antonia, who, though she was pockmarked and walleyed, nevertheless enjoyed a notorious reputation—indeed it was confidently proclaimed that no man had failed to go with her behind the river weeds at some time or other—shouted to Camilla:

"Hey there, you! What's the matter? What are you doing there skulking in the corner with a shawl tied round your head! You're crying, I wager. Look at her eyes; they look like a witch's. There's no sorrow lasts more than three days!"

Agapita knitted her eyebrows and muttered indistinctly to herself.

The old crones felt uneasy and lonesome since Demetrio's men had left. The men, too, in spite of their gossip and insults, lamented their departure since now they would have no one to bring them fresh meat every day. It is pleasant indeed to spend your time eating and drinking, and sleeping all day long in the cool shade of the rocks, while clouds ravel and unravel their fleecy threads on the blue shuttle of the sky.

"Look at them again. There they go!" María Antonia yelled. "Why, they look like toys."

Demetrio's men, riding their thin nags, could still be descried in the distance against the sapphire translucence of the sky, where the broken rocks and the chaparral melted into a single bluish smooth surface. Across the air a gust of hot wind bore the broken, faltering strains of "La Adelita," the revolutionary song, to the settlement. Camilla, who had come out when María Antonia shouted, could no longer control herself; she dived back into her hut, unable to restrain her tears and moaning. María Antonia burst into laughter and moved off.

"They've cast the evil eye on my daughter," Agapita said in perplexity. She pondered a while, then duly reached a decision. From a pole in the hut she took down a piece of strong leather which her husband used to hitch up the yoke. This pole stood between a picture of Christ and one of the Virgin. Agapita promptly twisted the leather and proceeded to administer a sound thrashing to Camilla in order to dispel the evil spirits.

Riding proudly on his horse, Demetrio felt like a new man. His eyes recovered their peculiar metallic brilliance, and the blood flowed, red and warm, through his coppery, pure-blooded Aztec cheeks.

The men threw out their chests as if to breathe the widening horizon, the immensity of the sky, the blue from the mountains and the fresh air, redolent with the various odors of the sierra. They spurred their horses to a gallop as if in that mad race they laid claims of possession to the earth. What man among them now remembered the stern chief of police, the growling policeman, or the conceited *cacique?* What man remembered his pitiful hut where he slaved away, always under the eyes of the owner or the ruthless and sullen foreman, always forced to rise before dawn, and to take up his shovel, basket, or goad, wearing himself out to earn a mere pitcher of *atole* and a handful of beans?

They laughed, they sang, they whistled, drunk with the sunlight, the air of the open spaces, the wine of life.

Meco, prancing forward on his horse, bared his white glistening teeth, joking and kicking up like a clown.

"Hey, Pancracio," he asked with utmost seriousness, "my wife writes me I've got another kid. How in hell is that? I ain't seen her since Madero was President."

"That's nothing," the other replied. "You just left her a lot of eggs to hatch for you!"

They all laughed uproariously. Only Meco, grave and aloof, sang in a voice horribly shrill:

"I gave her a penny
That wasn't enough.
I gave her a nickel
The wench wanted more.
We bargained. I asked
If a dime was enough
But she wanted a quarter.
By God! That was tough!
All wenches are fickle
And trumpery stuff!"

The sun, beating down upon them, dulled their minds and bodies and presently they were silent. All day long they rode through the canyon, up and down the steep, round hills, dirty and bald as a man's head, hill after hill in endless succession. At last, late in the afternoon, they descried several stone church towers in the heart of a bluish ridge, and, beyond, the white road with its curling spirals of dust and its gray telegraph poles.

They advanced toward the main road; in the distance they spied a figure of an Indian sitting on the embankment. They drew up to him. He proved to be an unfriendly looking old man, clad in rags; he was laboriously attempting to mend his leather sandals with the help of a dull knife. A burro loaded with fresh green grass stood by. Demetrio accosted him.

"What are you doing, Grandpa?"

"Gathering alfalfa for my cow."

"How many Federals are there around here?"

"Just a few: not more than a dozen, I reckon."

The old man grew communicative. He told them of many important rumors: Obregón was besieging Guadalajara, Torres was in complete control of the Potosí region, Natera ruled over Fresnillo.

"All right," said Demetrio, "you can go where you're headed for, see, but you be damn careful not to tell anyone you saw us, because if you do, I'll pump you full of lead. And I could track you down, even if you tried to hide in the pit of hell, see?"

"What do you say, boys?" Demetrio asked them as soon as the old man had disappeared.

"To hell with the *mochos!* We'll kill every blasted one of them!" they cried in unison.

Then they set to counting their cartridges and the hand grenades the Owl had made out of fragments of iron tubing and metal bed handles.

"Not much to brag about, but we'll soon trade them for rifles," Anastasio observed.

Anxiously they pressed forward, spurring the thin

flanks of their nags to a gallop. Demetrio's brisk, imperious tones of order brought them abruptly to a halt.

They dismounted by the side of a hill, protected by thick *huizache* trees. Without unsaddling their horses, each began to search for stones to serve as pillows.

Chapter 16

At midnight Demetrio Macías ordered the march to be resumed. The town was five or six miles away; the best plan was to take the soldiers by surprise, before reveille.

The sky was cloudy, with here and there a star shining. From time to time a flash of lightning crossed the sky with a red dart, illumining the far horizon.

Luis Cervantes asked Demetrio whether the success of the attack might not be better served by procuring a guide or leastways by ascertaining the topographic conditions of the town and the precise location of the soldiers' quarters.

"No," Demetrio answered, accompanying his smile with a disdainful gesture, "we'll simply fall on them when they least expect it; that's all there is to it, see? We've done it before all right, lots of times! Haven't you ever seen the squirrels stick their heads out of their holes when you poured in water? Well, that's how these lousy soldiers are going to feel. Do you see? They'll be frightened out of their wits the moment they hear our first shot. Then they'll slink out and stand as targets for us."

"Suppose the old man we met yesterday lied to us. Suppose there are fifty soldiers instead of twenty. Who knows but he's a spy sent out by the Federals!"

"Ha, Tenderfoot, frightened already, eh?" Anastasio Montáñez mocked.

"Sure! Handling a rifle and messing about with bandages are two different things," Pancracio observed.

"Well, that's enough talk, I guess," said Meco. "All we have to do is fight a dozen frightened rats."

"This fight won't convince our mothers that they

gave birth to men or whatever the hell you like. . . ." Manteca added.

When they reached the outskirts of the town, Venancio walked ahead and knocked at the door of a hut.

"Where's the soldiers' barracks?" he inquired of a man who came out barefoot, a ragged serape covering his body.

"Right there, just beyond the Plaza," he answered.

Since nobody knew where the city square was, Venancio made him walk ahead to show the way. Trembling with fear, the poor devil told them they were doing him a terrible wrong.

"I'm just a poor day laborer, sir; I've got a wife and a lot of kids."

"What the hell do you think I have, dogs?" Demetrio scowled. "I've got kids too, see?"

Then he commanded:

"You men keep quiet. Not a sound out of you! And walk down the middle of the street, single file."

The rectangular church cupola rose above the small houses.

"Here, gentlemen; there's the Plaza beyond the church. Just walk a bit further and there's the barracks."

He knelt down, then, imploring them to let him go, but Pancracio, without pausing to reply, struck him across the chest with his rifle and ordered him to proceed.

"How many soldiers are there?" Luis Cervantes asked.

"I don't want to lie to you, boss, but to tell you the truth, yes, sir, to tell you God's truth, there's a lot of them, a whole lot of 'em."

Luis Cervantes turned around to stare at Demetrio, who feigned momentary deafness.

They were soon in the city square.

A loud volley of rifle shots rang out, deafening them.

Demetrio's horse reared, staggered on its hind legs, bent its forelegs, and fell to the ground, kicking. The Owl uttered a piercing cry and fell from his horse which rushed madly to the center of the square.

Another volley: the guide threw up his arms and fell on his back without a sound.

With all haste, Anastasio Montáñez helped Demetrio up behind him on his horse; the others retreated, seeking shelter along the walls of the houses.

"Hey, men," said a workman sticking his head out of a large door, "go for 'em through the back of the chapel. They're all in there. Cut back through this street, then turn to the left; you'll reach an alley. Keep on going ahead until you hit the chapel."

As he spoke a fresh volley of pistol shots, directed from the neighboring roofs, fell like a rain about them.

"By God," the man said, "those ain't poisonous spiders; they're only townsmen scared of their own shadow. Come in here until they stop."

"How many of them are there?" asked Demetrio.

"There were only twelve of them. But last night they were scared out of their wits so they wired to the town beyond for help. I don't know how many of them there are now. Even if there are a hell of a lot of them, it doesn't cut any ice! Most of them aren't soldiers, you know, but drafted men; if just one of them starts mutinying, the rest will follow like sheep. My brother was drafted; they've got him there. I'll go along with you and signal to him; all of them will desert and follow you. Then we'll only have the officers to deal with! If you want to give me a gun or something. . . ."

"No more rifles left, brother. But I guess you can put these to some use," Anastasio Montáñez said, passing him two hand grenades.

The officer in command of the Federals was a young coxcomb of a captain with a waxed mustache and blond hair. As long as he felt uncertain about the strength of the assailants, he had remained extremely quiet and prudent; but now that they had driven the rebels back without allowing them a chance to fire a single shot, he waxed bold and brave. While the soldiers did not dare put out their heads beyond the pillars of the building, his own shadow stood against the pale clear dawn, exhibiting his well-built slender body and his officer's cape bellying in the breeze.

"Ha, I remember our *coup d'état!*"

His military career had consisted of the single adventure when, together with other students of the Officers' School, he was involved in the treacherous revolt of Féliz Díaz and Huerta against President Madero. Whenever the slightest insubordination arose, he invariably recalled his feat at the *Ciudadela.*

"Lieutenant Campos," he ordered emphatically, "take a dozen men and wipe out the bandits hiding there! The curs! They're only brave when it comes to guzzling meat and robbing a hencoop!"

A workingman appeared at the small door of the spiral staircase, announcing that the assailants were hidden in a corral where they might easily be captured. This message came from the citizens keeping watch on housetops.

"I'll go myself and get it over with!" the officer declared impetuously.

But he soon changed his mind. Before he had reached the door, he retraced his steps.

"Very likely they are waiting for more men and, of course, it would be wrong for me to abandon my post. Lieutenant Campos, go there yourself and capture them dead or alive. We'll shoot them at noon when everybody's coming out of church. Those bandits will see the example I'll set around here. But if you can't capture them, Lieutenant, kill them all. Don't leave a man of them alive, do you understand?"

In high good humor, he began pacing up and down the room, formulating the official despatch he would send off no later than today.

To His Honor the Minister for War,
General A. Blanquet,
Mexico City.

Sir:

I have the honor to inform your Excellency that on the morning of . . . a rebel army, five hundred strong, commanded by . . . attacked this town, which I am charged to defend. With such speed as the gravity of the situation called for, I fortified my post in the town. The battle lasted two hours. Despite the superiority of the enemy in men and equipment, I was able to defeat and rout them. Their casualties were twenty killed and a far greater number of wounded, judging from the trails of blood they left behind them as they retreated. I am pleased to state there was no casualty on our side. I have the honor to congratulate Your Excellency upon this new triumph for the Federal arms. Viva Presidente Huerta! Viva México!

"Well," the young captain mused, "I'll be promoted to major." He clasped his hands together, jubilant. At this precise moment, a detonation rang out. His ears buzzed, he—

Chapter 17

"If we get through the corral, we can make the alley, eh?" Demetrio asked.

"That's right," the workman answered. "Beyond the corral there's a house, then another corral, then there's a store."

Demetrio scratched his head, thoughtfully. This time his decision was immediate.

"Can you get hold of a crowbar or something like that to make a hole through the wall?"

"Yes, we'll get anything you want, but . . ."

"But what? Where can we get a crowbar?"

"Everything is right there. But it all belongs to the boss."

Without further ado, Demetrio strode into the shed which had been pointed out as the toolhouse.

It was all a matter of a few minutes. Once in the alley, hugging to the walls, they marched forward in single file until they reached the rear of the church. Now they had but a single fence and the rear wall of the chapel to scale.

"God's will be done!" Demetrio said to himself. He was the first to clamber over.

Like monkeys the others followed him, reaching the other side with bleeding, grimy hands. The rest was easy. The deep worn steps along the stonework made their ascent of the chapel wall swifter. The church vault hid them from the soldiers.

"Wait a moment, will you?" said the workman. "I'll go and see where my brother is; I'll let you know and then you'll get at the officers."

But no one paid the slightest attention to him.

For a second, Demetrio glanced at the soldiers'

black coats hanging on the wall, then at his own men, thick on the church tower behind the iron rail. He smiled with satisfaction and turning to his men said:

"Come on, now, boys!"

Twenty bombs exploded simultaneously in the midst of the soldiers who, awaking terrified out of their sleep, started up, their eyes wide open. But before they had realized their plight, twenty more bombs burst like thunder upon them leaving a scattering of men killed or maimed.

"Don't do that yet, for God's sake! Don't do it till I find my brother," the workman implored in anguish.

In vain an old sergeant harangued the soldiers, insulting them in the hope of rallying them. For they were rats, caught in a trap, no more, no less. Some of the soldiers, attempting to reach the small door by the staircase, fell to the ground pierced by Demetrio's shots. Others fell at the feet of these twenty-odd specters, with faces and breasts dark as iron, clad in long torn trousers of white cloth which fell to their leather sandals, scattering death and destruction below them. In the belfry, a few men struggled to emerge from the pile of dead who had fallen upon them.

"It's awful, Chief!" Luis Cervantes cried in alarm. "We've no more bombs left and we left our guns in the corral."

Smiling, Demetrio drew out a large shining knife. In the twinkling of an eye, steel flashed in every hand. Some knives were large and pointed, others wide as the palm of a hand, others heavy as bayonets.

"The spy!" Luis Cervantes cried triumphantly. "Didn't I tell you?"

"Don't kill me, Chief, please don't kill me," the old sergeant implored squirming at the feet of Demetrio, who stood over him, knife in hand. The victim raised his wrinkled Indian face; there was not a single gray hair in his head today. Demetrio recognized the spy who had lied to him the day before. Terrified, Luis Cervantes quickly averted his face. The steel blade went *crack, crack,* on the old man's ribs. He toppled backward, his arms spread, his eyes ghastly.

"Don't kill my brother, don't kill him, he's my brother!" the workman shouted in terror to Pancracio who was pursuing a soldier. But it was too late. With one thrust, Pancracio had cut his neck in half, and two streams of scarlet spurted from the wound.

"Kill the soldiers, kill them all!"

Pancracio and Manteca surpassed the others in the savagery of their slaughter, and finished up with the wounded. Montáñez, exhausted, let his arm fall; it hung limp to his side. A gentle expression still filled his glance; his eyes shone; he was naïve as a child, unmoral as a hyena.

"Here's one who's not dead yet," Quail shouted.

Pancracio ran up. The little blond captain with curled mustache turned pale as wax. He stood against the door to the staircase unable to muster enough strength to take another step.

Pancracio pushed him brutally to the edge of the corridor. A jab with his knee against the captain's thigh—then a sound not unlike a bag of stones falling from the top of the steeple on the porch of the church.

"My God, you've got no brains!" said Quail. "If I'd known what you were doing, I'd have kept him for myself. That was a fine pair of shoes you lost!"

Bending over them, the rebels stripped those among the soldiers who were best clad, laughing and joking as they despoiled them. Brushing back his long hair, that had fallen over his sweating forehead and covered his eyes, Demetrio said:

"Now let's get those city fellows!"

Chapter 18

On the day General Natera began his advance against the town of Zacatecas, Demetrio with a hundred men went to meet him at Fresnillo.

The leader received him cordially.

"I know who you are and the sort of men you bring. I heard about the beatings you gave the Federals from Tepic to Durango."

Natera shook hands with Demetrio effusively while Luis Cervantes said:

"With men like General Natera and Colonel Demetrio Macías, we'll cover our country with glory."

Demetrio understood the purpose of those words, after Natera had repeatedly addressed him as "Colonel."

Wine and beer were served; Demetrio and Natera drank many a toast. Luis Cervantes proposed: "The triumph of our cause, which is the sublime triumph of Justice, because our ideal—to free the noble, long-suffering people of Mexico—is about to be realized and because those men who have watered the earth with their blood and tears will reap the harvest which is rightfully theirs."

Natera fixed his cruel gaze on the orator, then turned his back on him to talk to Demetrio. Presently, one of Natera's officers, a young man with a frank open face, drew up to the table and stared insistently at Cervantes.

"Are you Luis Cervantes?"

"Yes. You're Solís, eh?"

"The moment you entered I thought I recognized you. Well, well, even now I can hardly believe my eyes!"

"It's true though!"

"Well, but . . . look here, let's have a drink, come along." Then:

"Hm," Solís went on, offering Cervantes a chair, "since when have you turned rebel?"

"I've been a rebel the last two months!"

"Oh, I see! That's why you speak with such faith and enthusiasm about things we all felt when we joined the revolution."

"Have you lost your faith or enthusiasm?"

"Look here, man, don't be surprised if I confide in you right off. I am so anxious to find someone intelligent among this crowd, that as soon as I get hold of a man like you I clutch at him as eagerly as I would at a glass of water, after walking mile after mile through a parched desert. But frankly, I think you should do the explaining first. I can't understand how a man who was correspondent of a Government newspaper during the Madero regime, and later editorial writer on a Conservative journal, who denounced us as bandits in the most fiery articles, is now fighting on our side."

"I tell you honestly: I have been converted," Cervantes answered.

"Are you absolutely convinced?"

Solís sighed, filled the glasses; they drank.

"What about you? Are you tired of the revolution?" asked Cervantes sharply.

"Tired? My dear fellow, I'm twenty-five years old and I'm fit as a fiddle! But am I disappointed? Perhaps!"

"You must have sound reasons for feeling that way."

"I hoped to find a meadow at the end of the road, I found a swamp. Facts are bitter; so are men. That bitterness eats your heart out; it is poison, dry rot. Enthusiasm, hope, ideals, happiness—vain dreams, vain dreams. . . . When that's over, you have a choice. Either you turn bandit, like the rest, or the timeservers will swamp you. . . ."

Cervantes writhed at his friend's words; his argument was quite out of place . . . painful. . . . To avoid being forced to take issue, he invited Solís to cite the circumstances that had destroyed his illusions.

"Circumstances? No—it's far less important than that. It's a host of silly, insignificant things that no one notices except yourself . . . a change of expression, eyes shining—lips curled in a sneer—the deep import of a phrase that is lost! Yet take these things together and they compose the mask of our race . . . terrible . . . grotesque . . . a race that awaits redemption!"

He drained another glass. After a long pause, he continued:

"You ask me why I am still a rebel? Well, the revolution is like a hurricane: if you're in it, you're not a man . . . you're a leaf, a dead leaf, blown by the wind."

Demetrio reappeared. Seeing him, Solís relapsed into silence.

"Come along," Demetrio said to Cervantes. "Come with me."

Unctuously, Solís congratulated Demetrio on the feats that had won him fame and the notice of Pancho Villa's northern division.

Demetrio warmed to his praise. Gratefully, he heard his prowess vaunted, though at times he found it difficult to believe he was the hero of the exploits the other narrated. But Solís' story proved so charming, so convincing, that before long he found himself repeating it as gospel truth.

"Natera is a genius!" Luis Cervantes said when they had returned to the hotel. "But Captain Solís is a nobody . . . a timeserver."

Demetrio Macías was too elated to listen to him.

"I'm a colonel, my lad! And you're my secretary!"

Demetrio's men made many acquaintances that evening; much liquor flowed to celebrate new friendships.

Of course men are not necessarily even tempered, nor is alcohol a good counselor; quarrels naturally ensued. Yet many differences that occurred were smoothed out in a friendly spirit, outside the saloons, restaurants, or brothels.

On the morrow, casualties were reported. Always a few dead. An old prostitute was found with a bullet through her stomach; two of Colonel Macías' new men lay in the gutter, slit from ear to ear.

Anastasio Montáñez carried an account of the events to his chief. Demetrio shrugged his shoulders.

"Bury them!" he said.

Chapter 19

"They're coming back!"

It was with amazement that the inhabitants of Fresnillo learned that the rebel attack on Zacatecas had failed completely.

"They're coming back!"

The rebels were a maddened mob, sunburnt, filthy, naked. Their high wide-brimmed straw hats hid their faces. The "high hats" came back as happily as they had marched forth a few days before, pillaging every hamlet along the road, every ranch, even the poorest hut.

"Who'll buy this thing?" one of them asked. He had carried his spoils long: he was tired. The sheen of the nickel on the typewriter, a new machine, attracted every glance. Five times that morning the Oliver had changed hands. The first sale netted the owner ten pesos; presently it had sold for eight; each time it changed hands, it was two pesos cheaper. To be sure, it was a heavy burden; nobody could carry it for more than a half-hour.

"I'll give you a quarter for it!" Quail said.

"Yours!" cried the owner, handing it over quickly, as though he feared Quail might change his mind. Thus for the sum of twenty-five cents, Quail was afforded the pleasure of taking it in his hands and throwing it with all his might against the wall.

It struck with a crash. This gave the signal to all who carried any cumbersome objects to get rid of them by smashing them against the rocks. Objects of all sorts, crystal, china, faïence, porcelain, flew through the air. Heavy, plated mirrors, brass candlesticks, fragile, delicate statues, Chinese vases, any object not readily convertible into cash fell by the wayside in fragments.

Demetrio did not share the untoward exaltation. After all, they were retreating defeated. He called Montáñez and Pancracio aside and said:

"These fellows have no guts. It's not so hard to take a town. It's like this. First, you open up, this way. . . ." He sketched a vast gesture, spreading his powerful arms. "Then you get close to them, like this. . . ." He brought his arms together, slowly. "Then slam! Bang! Whack! Crash!" He beat his hands against his chest.

Anastasio and Pancracio, convinced by this simple, lucid explanation answered:

"That's God's truth! They've no guts! That's the trouble with them!"

Demetrio's men camped in a corral.

"Do you remember Camilla?" Demetrio asked with a sigh as he settled on his back on the manure pile where the rest were already stretched out.

"Camilla? What girl do you mean, Demetrio?"

"The girl that used to feed me up there at the ranch!"

Anastasio made a gesture implying: "I don't care a damn about the women . . . Camilla or anyone else. . . ."

"I've not forgotten," Demetrio went on, drawing on his cigarette. "Yes, I was feeling like hell! I'd just finished drinking a glass of water. God, but it was cool. . . . 'Don't you want any more?' she asked me. I was half dead with fever . . . and all the time I saw that glass of water, blue . . . so blue . . . and I heard her little voice, 'Don't you want any more?' That voice tinkled in my ears like a silver hurdy-gurdy! Well, Pancracio, what about it? Shall we go back to the ranch?"

"Demetrio, we're friends, aren't we? Well then, listen. You may not believe it, but I've had a lot of experience with women. Women! Christ, they're all right for a while, granted! Though even that's going pretty far. Demetrio, you should see the scars they've given me . . . all over my body, not to speak of my soul! To hell with women. They're the devil, that's what they are! You may have noticed I steer clear of them. You know why. And don't think I don't know what I'm talking about. I've had a hell of a lot of experience and that's no lie!"

"What do you say, Pancracio? When are we going back to the ranch?" Demetrio insisted, blowing gray clouds of tobacco smoke into the air.

"Say the day, I'm game. You know I left my woman there too!"

"Your woman, hell!" Quail said, disgruntled and sleepy.

"All right, then, our woman! It's a good thing you're kindhearted so we all can enjoy her when you bring her over," Manteca murmured.

"That's right, Pancracio, bring one-eyed María Antonia. We're all getting pretty cold around here," Meco shouted from a distance.

The crowd broke into peals of laughter. Pancracio and Manteca vied with each other in calling forth oaths and obscenity.

Chapter 20

"Villa is coming!"

The news spread like lightning. Villa—the magic word! The Great Man, the salient profile, the unconquerable warrior who, even at a distance, exerts the fascination of a reptile, a boa constrictor.

"Our Mexican Napoleon!" exclaimed Luis Cervantes.

"Yes! The Aztec Eagle! He buried his beak of steel in the head of Huerta the serpent!" Solís, Natera's chief of staff, remarked somewhat ironically, adding: "At least, that's how I expressed it in a speech I made at Ciudad Juárez!"

The two sat at the bar of the saloon, drinking beer. The "high hats," wearing mufflers around their necks and thick rough leather shoes on their feet, ate and drank endlessly. Their gnarled hands loomed across table, across bar. All their talk was of Villa and his men. The tales Natera's followers related won gasps of astonishment from Demetrio's men. Villa! Villa's battles! Ciudad Juárez . . . Tierra Blanca . . . Chihuahua . . . Torreón. . . .

The bare facts, the mere citing of observation and experience meant nothing. But the real story, with its extraordinary contrasts of high exploits and abysmal cruelties was quite different. Villa, indomitable lord of the sierra, the eternal victim of all governments . . . Villa tracked, hunted down like a wild beast . . . Villa the reincarnation of the old legend; Villa as Providence, the bandit, that passes through the world armed with the blazing torch of an ideal: to rob the rich and give to the poor. It was the poor who built up and imposed a legend about him which Time itself was to increase and embellish as a shining example from generation to generation.

"Look here, friend," one of Natera's men told Anastasio, "if General Villa takes a fancy to you, he'll give you a ranch on the spot. But if he doesn't, he'll shoot you down like a dog! God! You ought to see Villa's troops! They're all northerners and dressed like lords! You ought to see their wide-brimmed Texas hats and their brand-new outfits and their four-dollar shoes, imported from the U.S.A."

As they retailed the wonders of Villa and his men, Natera's men gazed at one another ruefully, aware that their own hats were rotten from sunlight and moisture, that their own shirts and trousers were tattered and barely fit to cover their grimy, lousy bodies.

"There's no such a thing as hunger up there. They carry boxcars full of oxen, sheep, cows! They've got cars full of clothing, trains full of guns, ammunition, food enough to make a man burst!"

Then they spoke of Villa's airplanes.

"Christ, those planes! You know when they're close to you, be damned if you know what the hell they are! They look like small boats, you know, or tiny rafts . . . and then pretty soon they begin to rise, making a hell of a row. Something like an automobile going sixty miles an hour. Then they're like great big birds that don't even seem to move sometimes. But there's a joker! The Goddamn things have got some American fellow inside with hand grenades by the thousand. Now you try and figure what that means! The fight is on, see? You know how a farmer feeds corn to his chickens, huh? Well, the American throws his lead bombs at the enemy just like that. Pretty soon the whole damn field is nothing but a graveyard . . . dead men all over the dump . . . dead men here . . . dead men there . . . dead men everywhere!"

Anastasio Montáñez questioned the speaker more particularly. It was not long before he realized that all this high praise was hearsay and that not a single man in Natera's army had ever laid eyes on Villa.

"Well, when you get down to it, I guess it doesn't mean so much! No man's got much more guts than any other man, if you ask me. All you need to be a good fighter is pride, that's all. I'm not a professional soldier even though I'm dressed like hell, but let me tell you. I'm not forced to do this kind of bloody job, because I own . . ."

"Because I own over twenty oxen, whether you believe it or not!" Quail said, mocking Anastasio.

Chapter 21

The firing lessened, then slowly died out. Luis Cervantes, who had been hiding amid a heap of ruins at the fortification on the crest of the hill, made bold to show his face. How he had managed to hang on, he did not know. Nor did he know when Demetrio and his men had disappeared. Suddenly he had found himself alone; then, hurled back by an avalanche of infantry, he fell from his saddle; a host of men trampled over him until he rose from the ground and a man on horseback hoisted him up behind him. After a few moments, horse and riders fell. Left without rifle, revolver, or arms of any kind, Cervantes found himself lost in the midst of white smoke and whistling bullets. A hole amid a debris of crumbling stone offered a refuge of safety.

"Hello, partner!"

"Luis, how are you?"

"The horse threw me. They fell upon me. Then they took my gun away. You see, they thought I was dead. There was nothing I could do!" Luis Cervantes explained apologetically. Then:

"Nobody threw me down," Solís said. "I'm here because I like to play safe."

The irony in Solís' voice brought a blush to Cervantes' cheek.

"By God, that chief of yours is a man!" Solís said. "What daring, what assurance! He left me gasping—and a hell of a lot of other men with more experience than me, too!"

Luis Cervantes vouchsafed no answer.

"What! Weren't you there? Oh, I see! You found a nice place for yourself at the right time. Come here,

Luis, I'll explain; let's go behind that rock. From this meadow to the foot of the hill, there's no road save this path below. To the right, the incline is too sharp; you can't do anything there. And it's worse to the left; the ascent is so dangerous that a second's hesitation means a fall down those rocks and a broken neck at the end of it. All right! A number of men from Moya's brigade who went down to the meadow decided to attack the enemy's trenches the first chance they got. The bullets whizzed about us, the battle raged on all sides. For a time they stopped firing, so we thought they were being attacked from behind. We stormed their trenches—look, partner, look at that meadow! It's thick with corpses! Their machine guns did that for us. They mowed us down like wheat; only a handful escaped. Those Goddamned officers went white as a sheet; even though we had reinforcements they were afraid to order a new charge. That was when Demetrio Macías plunged in. Did he wait for orders? Not he! He just shouted:

"'Come on, boys! Let's go for them!'

"'Damn fool!' I thought. 'What the hell does he think he's doing!'

"The officers, surprised, said nothing. Demetrio's horse seemed to wear eagle's claws instead of hoofs, it soared so swiftly over the rocks. 'Come on! Come on!' his men shouted, following him like wild deer, horses and men welded into a mad stampede. Only one young fellow stepped wild and fell headlong into the pit. In a few seconds the others appeared at the top of the hill, storming the trenches and killing the Federals by the thousand. With his rope, Demetrio lassoed the machine guns and carried them off, like a bull herd throwing a steer. Yet his success could not last much longer, for the Federals were far stronger in numbers and could easily have destroyed Demetrio and his men. But we took advantage of their confusion, we rushed upon them and they soon cleared out of their position. That chief of yours is a wonderful soldier!"

Standing on the crest of the hill, they could easily sight one side of the Bufa peak. Its highest crag spread out like the feathered head of a proud Aztec king. The three-hundred-foot slope was literally covered with dead, their hair matted, their clothes clotted with grime and blood. A host of ragged women, vultures of prey, ranged over the tepid bodies of the dead, stripping one man bare, despoiling another, robbing from a third his dearest possessions.

Amid clouds of white rifle smoke and the dense black vapors of flaming buildings, houses with wide doors and windows bolted shone in the sunlight. The streets seemed to be piled upon one another, or wound picturesquely about fantastic corners, or set to scale the hills nearby. Above the graceful cluster of houses, rose the lithe columns of a warehouse and the towers and cupola of the church.

"How beautiful the revolution! Even in its most barbarous aspect it is beautiful," Solís said with deep feeling. Then a vague melancholy seized him, and speaking low:

"A pity what remains to do won't be as beautiful! We must wait a while, until there are no men left to fight on either side, until no sound of shot rings through the air save from the mob as carrion-like it falls upon the booty; we must wait until the psychology of our race, condensed into two words, shines clear and luminous as a drop of water: *Robbery! Murder!* What a colossal failure we would make of it, friend, if we, who offer our enthusiasm and lives to crush a wretched tyrant, became the builders of a monstrous edifice holding one hundred or two hundred thousand monsters of exactly the same sort. People without ideals! A tyrant folk! Vain bloodshed!"

Large groups of Federals pushed up the hill, fleeing from the "high hats." A bullet whistled past them, singing as it sped. After his speech, Alberto Solís stood lost in thought, his arms crossed. Suddenly, he took fright.

"I'll be damned if I like these plaguey mosquitoes!" he said. "Let's get away from here!"

So scornfully Luis Cervantes smiled that Solís sat down on a rock quite calm, bewildered. He smiled. His gaze roved as he watched the spirals of smoke from the rifles, the dust of roofs crumbling from houses as they fell before the artillery. He believed he discerned the symbol of the revolution in these clouds of dust and smoke that climbed upward together, met at the crest of the hill and, a moment after, were lost. . . .

"By heaven, now I see what it all means!"

He sketched a vast gesture, pointing to the station. Locomotives belched huge clouds of black dense smoke rising in columns; the trains were overloaded with fugitives who had barely managed to escape from the captured town.

Suddenly he felt a sharp blow in the stomach. As though his legs were putty, he rolled off the rock. His ears buzzed . . . Then darkness . . . silence . . . eternity. . . .

Part Two

Demetrio, nonplussed, scratched his head: "Look here, don't ask me any more questions. . . . You gave me the eagle I wear on my hat, didn't you? All right then; you just tell me: 'Demetrio, do this or do that,' and that's all there is to it."

Chapter 1

To champagne, that sparkles and foams as the beaded bubbles burst at the brim of the glass, Demetrio preferred the native tequila, limpid and fiery.

The soldiers sat in groups about the tables in the restaurant, ragged men, filthy with sweat, dirt and smoke, their hair matted, wild, disheveled.

"I killed two colonels," one man clamored in a guttural harsh voice. He was a small fat fellow, with embroidered hat and chamois coat, wearing a light purple handkerchief about his neck.

"They were so Goddamned fat they couldn't even run. By God, I wish you could have seen them, tripping and stumbling at every step they took, climbing up the hill, red as tomatoes, their tongues hanging out like hounds. 'Don't run so fast, you lousy beggars!' I called after them. 'I'm not so fond of frightened geese—stop, you bald-headed bastards: I won't harm you! You needn't worry!' By God, they certainly fell for it. *Pop, pop!* One shot for each of them, and a well-earned rest for a pair of poor sinners, be damned to them!"

"I couldn't get a single one of their generals!" said a swarthy man who sat in one corner between the wall and the bar, holding his rifle between his outstretched legs. "I sighted one: a fellow with a hell of a lot of gold plastered all over him. His gold chevrons shone like a Goddamned sunset. And I let him go by, fool that I was. He took off his handkerchief and waved it. I stood there with my mouth wide open like a fool! Then I ducked and he started shooting, bullet after bullet. I let him kill a poor *cargador.* Then I said: 'My turn, now! Holy Virgin, Mother of God! Don't let me miss this son of a bitch.' But, by Christ, he disappeared. He was riding a hell of a fine nag; he went by me like lightning! There was another poor fool coming up the road. He got it and turned the prettiest somersault you ever saw!"

Talk flew from lip to lip, each soldier vying with his fellow, snatching the words from the other's mouth. As they declaimed passionately, women with olive, swarthy skins, bright eyes, and teeth of ivory, with revolvers at their waists, cartridge-belts across their breasts, and broad Mexican hats on their heads, wove their way like stray street curs in and out among groups. A vulgar wench, with rouged cheeks and dark brown arms and neck, gave a great leap and landed on the bar near Demetrio's table.

He turned his head toward her and literally collided with a pair of lubric eyes under a narrow forehead and thick, straight hair, parted in the middle.

The door opened wide. Anastasio, Pancracio, Quail, and Meco filed in, dazed.

Anastasio uttered a cry of surprise and stepped forward to shake hands with the little fat man wearing a *charro* suit and a lavender bandanna. A pair of old friends, met again. So warm was their embrace, so tightly they clutched each other that the blood rushed to their heads, they turned purple.

"Look here, Demetrio, I want the honor of introducing you to Blondie. He's a real friend, you know. I love him like a brother. You must get to know him, Chief, he's a man! Do you remember that damn jail at Escobedo, where we stayed together for over a year?"

Without removing his cigar from his lips, Demetrio, buried in a sullen silence amid the bustle and uproar, offered his hand and said:

"I'm delighted to meet you!"

"So your name is Demetrio Macías?" the girl asked suddenly. Seated on the bar, she swung her legs; at every swing, the toes of her shoes touched Demetrio's back.

"Yes: I'm Demetrio Macías!" he said, scarcely turning toward her.

Indifferently, she continued to swing her legs, displaying her blue stockings with ostentation.

"Hey, War Paint, what are you doing here? Step down and have a drink!" said the man called Blondie.

The girl accepted readily and boldly thrust her way through the crowd to a chair facing Demetrio.

"So you're the famous Demetrio Macías, the hero of Zacatecas?" the girl asked.

Demetrio bowed assent, while Blondie, laughing, said:

"You're a wise one, War Paint. You want to sport a general!"

Without understanding Blondie's words, Demetrio raised his eyes to hers; they gazed at each other like two dogs sniffing one another with distrust. Demetrio could not resist her furiously provocative glances; he was forced to lower his eyes.

From their seats, some of Natera's officers began to hurl obscenities at War Paint. Without paying the slightest attention, she said:

"General Natera is going to hand you out a little general's eagle. Put it here and shake on it, boy!"

She stuck out her hand at Demetrio and shook it with the strength of a man. Demetrio, melting to the congratulations raining down upon him, ordered champagne.

"I don't want no more to drink," Blondie said to the waiter, "I'm feeling sick. Just bring me some ice water."

"I want something to eat," said Pancracio. "Bring me anything you've got but don't make it chili or beans!"

Officers kept coming in; presently the restaurant was crowded. Small stars, bars, eagles and insignia of every sort or description dotted their hats. They wore wide silk bandannas around their necks, large diamond rings on their fingers, large heavy gold watch chains across their breasts.

"Here, waiter," Blondie cried, "I ordered ice water. And I'm not begging for it either, see? Look at this bunch of bills. I'll buy you, your wife, and all you possess, see? Don't tell me there's none left—I don't care a damn about that! It's up to you to find some way to get it and Goddamned quick, too. I don't like to play about; I get mad when I'm crossed. . . . By God, didn't I tell you I wouldn't stand for any backchat? You won't bring it to me, eh? Well, take this. . . ."

A heavy blow sent the waiter reeling to the floor.

"That's the sort of man I am, General Macías! I'm clean-shaven, eh? Not a hair on my chin? Do you know why? Well, I'll tell you! You see I get mad easy as hell; and when there's nobody to pick on, I pull my hair until my temper passes. If I hadn't pulled my beard hair by hair, I'd have died a long time ago from sheer anger!"

"It does you no good to go to pieces when you're angry," a man affirmed earnestly from below a hat that covered his head as a roof does a house. "When I was up at Torreón I killed an old lady who refused to sell me some enchiladas. She was angry, I can tell you; I got no enchiladas but I felt satisfied anyhow!"

"I killed a storekeeper at Parral because he gave me some change and there were two Huerta bills in it," said a man with a star on his hat and precious stones on his black, calloused hands.

"Down in Chihuahua I killed a man because I always saw him sitting at the table whenever I went to eat. I hated the looks of him so I just killed him! What the hell could I do!"

"Hmm! I killed. . . ."

The theme is inexhaustible.

By dawn, when the restaurant was wild with joy and the floor dotted with spittle, young painted girls from the suburbs had mingled freely among the dark northern women. Demetrio pulled out his jeweled gold watch, asking Anastasio Montáñez to tell him the time.

Anastasio glanced at the watch, then, poking his head out of a small window, gazed at the starry sky.

"The Pleiades are pretty low in the west. I guess it won't be long now before daybreak. . . ."

Outside the restaurant, the shouts, laughter and song of the drunkards rang through the air. Men galloped wildly down the streets, the hoofs of their horses hammering on the sidewalks. From every quarter of the town pistols spoke, guns belched. Demetrio and the girl called War Paint staggered tipsily hand in hand down the center of the street, bound for the hotel.

Chapter 2

"What damned fools," said War Paint convulsed with laughter! "Where the hell do you come from? . . . Soldiers don't sleep in hotels and inns any more. . . . Where do you come from? You just go anywhere you like and pick a house that pleases you, see. When you go there, make yourself at home and don't ask anyone for anything. What the hell is the use of the revolution? Who's it for? For the folks who live in towns? We're the city folk now, see? Come on, Pancracio, hand me your bayonet. Damn these rich people, they lock up everything they've got!"

She dug the steel point through the crack of a drawer and, pressing on the hilt, broke the lock, opened the splinted cover of a writing desk. Anastasio, Pancracio and War Paint plunged their hands into a mass of post cards, photographs, pictures and papers, scattering them all over the rug. Finding nothing he wanted, Pancracio gave vent to his anger by kicking a framed photograph into the air with the toe of his shoe. It smashed on the candelabra in the center of the room.

They pulled their empty hands out of the heap of paper, cursing. But War Paint was of sterner stuff; tirelessly she continued to unlock drawer after drawer without failing to investigate a single spot. In their absorption, they did not notice a small gray velvet-covered box which rolled silently across the floor, coming to a stop at Luis Cervantes' feet.

Demetrio, lying on the rug, seemed to be asleep; Cervantes, who had watched everything with profound indifference, pulled the box closer to him with his foot, and stooping to scratch his ankle, swiftly picked it up. Something gleamed up at him, dazzling. It was two pure-water diamonds mounted in filigreed platinum. Hastily he thrust them inside his coat pocket.

When Demetrio awoke, Cervantes said:

"General, look at the mess these boys have made here. Don't you think it would be advisable to forbid this sort of thing?"

"No. It's about their only pleasure after putting their bellies up as targets for the enemy's bullets."

"Yes, of course, General, but they could do it somewhere else. You see, this sort of thing hurts our prestige, and worse, our cause!"

Demetrio leveled his eagle eyes at Cervantes. He drummed with his fingernails against his teeth, absent-mindedly. Then:

"Come along, now, don't blush," he said. "You can talk like that to someone else. We know what's mine is mine, what's yours is yours. You picked the box, all right; I picked my gold watch; all right too!"

His words dispelled any pretense. Both of them, in perfect harmony, displayed their booty.

War Paint and her companions were ransacking the rest of the house. Quail entered the room with a twelve-year-old girl upon whose forehead and arms were already marked copper-colored spots. They stopped short, speechless with surprise as they saw the books lying in piles on the floor, chairs and tables, the large mirrors thrown to the ground, smashed, the huge albums and the photographs torn into shreds, the furniture, *objets d'art* and bric-a-brac broken. Quail held his breath, his avid eyes scouring the room for booty.

Outside, in one corner of the patio, lost in dense clouds of suffocating smoke, Manteca was boiling corn on the cob, feeding his fire with books and paper that made the flames leap wildly through the air.

"Hey!" Quail shouted. "Look what I found. A fine sweat-cover for my mare."

With a swift pull he wrenched down a hanging, which fell over a handsomely carved upright chair.

"Look, look at all these naked women!" Quail's little companion cried, enchanted at a de luxe edition of Dante's *Divine Comedy*. "I like this; I think I'll take it along."

She began to tear out the illustrations which pleased her most.

Demetrio crossed the room and sat down beside Luis Cervantes. He ordered some beer, handed one bottle up to his secretary, downed his own bottle at one gulp. Then, drowsily, he half closed his eyes, and soon fell sound asleep.

"Hey!" a man called to Pancracio from the threshold. "When can I see your general?"

"You can't see him. He's got a hangover this morning. What the hell do you want?"

"I want to buy some of those books you're burning."

"I'll sell them to you myself."

"How much do you want for them?"

Pancracio frowned in bewilderment.

"Give me a nickel for those with pictures, see. I'll give you the rest for nothing if you buy all those with pictures."

The man returned with a large basket to carry away the books. . . .

"Come on, Demetrio, come on, you pig, get up! Look who's here! It's Blondie. You don't know what a fine man he is!"

"I like you very much, General Macías, and I like the way you do things. So if it's all right, I'd like very much to serve under you!"

"What's your rank?" Demetrio asked him.

"I'm a captain, General."

"All right, you can serve with me now. I'll make

you major. How's that?"

Blondie was a round little fellow, with waxed mustache. When he laughed, his blue eyes disappeared mischievously between his forehead and his fat cheeks. He had been a waiter at "El Mónico," in Chihuahua; now he proudly wore three small brass bars, the insignia of his rank in the Northern Division.

Blondie showered eulogy after eulogy on Demetrio and his men; this proved sufficient reason for bringing out a fresh case of beer, which was finished in short order.

Suddenly War Paint reappeared in the middle of the room, wearing a beautiful silk dress covered with exquisite lace.

"You forgot the stockings," Blondie shouted, shaking with laughter. Quail's girl also burst out laughing. But War Paint did not care. She shrugged her shoulders indifferently, sat down on the floor, kicked off her white satin slippers, and wiggled her toes happily, giving their muscles a freedom welcome after their tight confinement in the slippers. She said:

"Hey, you, Pancracio, go and get me my blue stockings . . . they're with the rest of my plunder."

Soldiers and their friends, companions and veterans of other campaigns, began to enter in groups of twos and threes. Demetrio, growing excited, began to narrate in detail his most notable feats of arms.

"What the hell is that noise?" he asked in surprise as he heard string and brass instruments tuning up in the patio.

"General Demetrio Macías," Luis Cervantes said solemnly, "it's a banquet all of your old friends and followers are giving in your honor to celebrate your victory at Zacatecas and your well-merited promotion to the rank of general!"

Chapter 3

"General Macías, I want you to meet my future wife," Luis Cervantes said with great emphasis as he led a beautiful girl into the dining room.

They all turned to look at her. Her large blue eyes grew wide in wonder. She was barely fourteen. Her skin was like a rose, soft, pink, fresh; her hair was very fair; the expression in her eyes was partly impish curiosity, partly a vague childish fear. Perceiving that Demetrio eyed her like a beast of prey, Luis Cervantes congratulated himself.

They made room for her between Luis Cervantes and Blondie, opposite Demetrio.

Bottles of tequila, dishes of cut glass, bowls, porcelains and vases lay scattered over the table indiscriminately. Meco, carrying a box of beer upon his shoulders, came in cursing and sweating.

"You don't know this fellow Blondie yet," said War Paint, noticing the persistent glances he was casting at Luis Cervantes' bride. "He's a smart fellow, I can tell you, and he never misses a trick."

She gazed at him lecherously, adding:

"That's why I don't like to see him close, even on a photograph!"

The orchestra struck up a raucous march as though they were playing at a bullfight. The soldiers roared with joy.

"What fine tripe, General; I swear I haven't tasted the like of it in all my life," Blondie said, as he began to reminisce about "El Mónico" at Chihuahua.

"You really like it, Blondie?" responded Demetrio. "Go ahead, call for more, eat your bellyful."

"It's just the way I like it," Anastasio chimed in.

"Yes, I like good food! But nothing really tastes good to you unless you belch!"

The noise of mouths being filled, of ravenous feeding followed. All drank copiously. At the end of the dinner, Luis Cervantes rose, holding a champagne glass in one hand, and said:

"General . . ."

"Ho!" War Paint interrupted. "This speech-making business isn't for me; I'm all against it. I'll go out to the corral since there's no more eating here."

Presenting Demetrio with a black velvet-covered box containing a small brass eagle, Luis Cervantes made a toast which no one understood but everyone applauded enthusiastically. Demetrio took the insignia in his hands; and with flushed face, and eyes shining, declared with great candor:

"What in hell am I going to do with this buzzard!"

"Compadre," Anastasio Montáñez said in a tremulous voice. "I ain't got much to tell you. . . ."

Whole minutes elapsed between his words; the cursed words would not come to Anastasio. His face, coated with filth, unwashed for days, turned crimson, shining with perspiration. Finally he decided to finish his toast at all costs. "Well, I ain't got much to tell you, except that we are pals. . . ."

Then, since everyone had applauded at the end of Luis Cervantes' speech, Anastasio, having finished, made a sign, and the company clapped their hands in great gravity.

But everything turned out for the best, since his awkwardness inspired others. Manteca and Quail stood up and made their toasts, too. When Meco's turn came, War Paint rushed in shouting jubilantly, attempting to drag a splendid black horse into the dining room.

"My booty! My booty!" she cried, patting the superb animal on the neck. It resisted every effort she made until a strong jerk of the rope and a sudden lash brought it in prancing smartly. The soldiers, half drunk, stared at the beast with ill-disguised envy.

"I don't know what the hell this she-devil's got, but she always beats everybody to it," cried Blondie. "She's been the same ever since she joined us at Tierra Blanca!"

"Hey, Pancracio, bring me some alfalfa for my horse," War Paint commanded crisply, throwing the horse's rope to one of the soldiers.

Once more they filled their glasses. Many a head hung low with fatigue or drunkenness. Most of the company, however, shouted with glee, including Luis Cervantes' girl. She had spilled all her wine on a handkerchief and looked all about her with blue wondering eyes.

"Boys," Blondie suddenly screamed, his shrill, guttural voice dominating the mall, "I'm tired of living; I feel like killing myself right now. I'm sick and tired of War Paint and this other little angel from heaven won't even look at me!"

Luis Cervantes saw that the last remark was addressed to his bride; with great surprise he realized that it was not Demetrio's foot he had noticed close to the girl's, but Blondie's. He was boiling with indignation.

"Keep your eye on me, boys," Blondie went on, gun in hand. "I'm going to shoot myself right in the forehead!"

He aimed at the large mirror on the opposite wall which gave back his whole body in reflection. He took careful aim. . . .

"Don't move, War Paint."

The bullet whizzed by, grazing War Paint's hair. The mirror broke into large jagged fragments. She did not even so much as blink.

Chapter 4

Late in the afternoon Luis Cervantes rubbed his eyes and sat up. He had been sleeping on the hard pavement, close to the trunk of a fruit tree. Anastasio, Pancracio and Quail slept nearby, breathing heavily.

His lips were swollen, his nose dry and cold. There were bloodstains on his hands and shirt. At once he recalled what had taken place. Soon he rose to his feet and made for one of the bedrooms. He pushed at the door several times without being able to force it open. For a few minutes he stood there, hesitating.

No—he had not dreamed it. Everything had really occurred just as he recalled it. He had left the table with his bride and taken her to the bedroom, but just as he was closing the door, Demetrio staggered after them and made one leap toward them. Then War Paint dashed in after Demetrio and began to struggle with him. Demetrio, his eyes white-hot, his lips covered with long blond hairs, looked for the bride, in despair. But War Paint pushed him back vigorously.

"What the hell is the matter with you? What the hell are you trying to do?" he demanded, furious.

War Paint put her leg between his, twisted it suddenly, and Demetrio fell to the ground outside of the bedroom. He rose, raging.

"Help! Help! He's going to kill me!" she cried, seizing Demetrio's wrist and turning the gun aside. The bullet hit the floor. War Paint continued to shriek. Anastasio disarmed Demetrio from behind.

Demetrio, standing like a furious bull in the middle of the arena, cast fierce glances at all the bystanders, Luis Cervantes, Anastasio, Manteca, and the others.

"Goddamn you! You've taken my gun away!

Christ! As if I needed any gun to beat the hell out of you."

Flinging out his arms, beating and pummeling, he felled everyone within reach. Down they rolled like tenpins. Then, after that, Luis Cervantes could remember nothing more. Perhaps his bride, terrified by all these brutes, had wisely vanished and hidden herself.

"Perhaps this bedroom communicates with the living room and I can go in through there," he thought, standing at the threshold. At the sound of his footsteps, War Paint woke up. She lay on the rug close to Demetrio at the foot of a couch filled with alfalfa and corn where the black horse had fed.

"What are you looking for? Oh, hell, I know what you want! Shame on *you!* Why, I had to lock up your sweetheart because I couldn't struggle any more against this damned Demetrio. Take the key, it's lying on that table, there!"

Luis Cervantes searched in vain all over the house.

"Come on, tell me all about your girl."

Nervously, Luis Cervantes continued to look for the key.

"Come on, don't be in such a hurry, I'll give it to you. Come along, tell me; I like to hear about these things, you know. That girl is your kind, she's not a country person like us."

"I've nothing to say. She's my girl and we're going to get married, that's all."

"Ho! Ho! Ho! You're going to marry her, eh? Trying to teach your grandmother to suck eggs, eh? Why, you fool, any place you just manage to get to for the first time in your life, I've left a hundred miles behind me, see. I've cut my wisdom teeth. It was Meco and Manteca who took the girl from her home: I knew that all the time. You just gave them something so as to have her yourself, gave them a pair of cuff links . . . or a miraculous picture of some Virgin . . . Am I right? Sure,

I am! There aren't so many people in the world who know what's what, but I reckon you'll meet up with a few before you die!"

War Paint got up to give him the key but she could not find it either. She was much surprised. Quickly, she ran to the bedroom door and peered through the keyhole, standing motionless until her eye grew accustomed to the darkness within. Without drawing away, she said:

"You damned Blondie. Son of a bitch! Come here a minute, look!"

She went away laughing.

"Didn't I tell them all I'd never seen a smarter fellow in all my life!"

The following morning, War Paint watched for the moment when Blondie left the bedroom to feed his horses. . . .

"Come on, Angel Face. Run home quick!"

The blue-eyed girl, with a face like a Madonna, stood naked save for her chemise and stockings. War Paint covered her with Manteca's lousy blanket, took her by the hand and led her to the street.

"God, I'm happy," War Paint cried. "I'm crazy . . . about Blondie . . . now."

Chapter

Like neighing colts, playful when the rainy season begins, Demetrio's men galloped through the sierra.

"To Moyahua, boys. Let's go to Demetrio Macías' country!"

"To the country of Mónico the *cacique!*"

The landscape grew clearer; the sun margined the diaphanous sky with a fringe of crimson. Like the bony shoulders of immense sleeping monsters, the chains of mountains rose in the distance. Crags there were like heads of colossal native idols; others like giants' faces, their grimaces awe-inspiring or grotesque, calling forth a smile or a shudder at a presentment of mystery.

Demetrio Macías rode at the head of his men; behind him the members of his staff: Colonel Anastasio Montáñez, Lieutenant-Colonel Pancracio, Majors Luis Cervantes and Blondie. Still further behind came War Paint with Venancio, who paid her many compliments and recited the despairing verses of Antonio Plaza. As the sun's rays began to slip from the housetops, they made their entrance into Moyahua, four abreast, to the sound of the bugle. The roosters' chorus was deafening, dogs barked their alarm, but not a living soul stirred on the streets.

War Paint spurred her black horse and with one jump was abreast with Demetrio. They rode forward, elbow to elbow. She wore a silk dress and heavy gold earrings. Proudly her pale blue gown deepened her olive skin and the coppery spots on her face and arms. Riding astride, she had pulled her skirts up to her knees; her stockings showed, filthy and full of runs. She wore a gun at her side, a cartridge belt hung over the pommel of her saddle.

Demetrio was also dressed in his best clothes. His broad-brimmed hat was richly embroidered; his leather trousers were tight-fitting and adorned with silver buttons; his coat was embroidered with gold thread.

There was a sound of doors being beaten down and forced open. The soldiers had already scattered through the town, to gather together ammunition and saddles from everywhere.

"We're going to bid Mónico good morning," Demetrio said gravely, dismounting and tossing his bridle to one of his men. "We're going to have breakfast with Don Mónico, who's a particular friend of mine. . . ."

The general's staff smiled . . . a sinister, malign smile. . . .

Making their spurs ring against the pavement, they walked toward a large pretentious house, obviously that of a *cacique*.

"It's closed airtight," Anastasio Montáñez said, pushing the door with all his might.

"That's all right. I'll open it," Pancracio answered, lowering his rifle and pointing it at the lock.

"No, no," Demetrio said, "knock first."

Three blows with the butt of the rifle. Three more. No answer. Pancracio disobeys orders. He fires, smashing the lock. The door opens. Behind, a confusion of skirts and children's bare legs rushing to and fro, pell-mell.

"I want wine. Hey, there: wine!" Demetrio cries in an imperious voice, pounding heavily on a table.

"Sit down, boys."

A lady peeps out, another, a third; from among black skirts, the heads of frightened children. One of the women, trembling, walks toward a cupboard and, taking out some glasses and a bottle, serves wine.

"What arms have you?" Demetrio demands harshly.

"Arms, arms . . .?" the lady answers, a taste of ashes on her tongue. "What arms do you expect us to have! We are respectable, lonely old ladies!"

"Lonely, eh! Where's Señor Mónico?"

"Oh, he's not here, gentlemen, I assure you! We merely rent the house from him, you see. We only know him by name!"

Demetrio orders his men to search the house.

"No, please don't. We'll bring you whatever we have ourselves, but please for God's sake, don't do anything cruel. We're spinsters, lone women . . . perfectly respectable. . . ."

"Spinsters, hell! What about these kids here?" Pancracio interrupts brutally. "Did they spring from the earth?"

The women disappear hurriedly, to return with an old shotgun, covered with dust and cobwebs, and a pistol with rusty broken springs.

Demetrio smiles.

"All right, then, let's see the money. . . ."

"Money? Money? But what money do you think a couple of spinsters have? Spinsters alone in the world. . . ?"

They glance up in supplication at the nearest soldier; but they are seized with horror. For they have just seen the Roman soldier who crucified Our Lord in the *Via Crucis* of the parish! They have seen Pancracio!

Demetrio repeats his order to search.

Once again the women disappear to return this time with a moth-eaten wallet containing a few Huerta bills.

Demetrio smiles and without further delay calls to his men to come in. Like hungry dogs who have sniffed their meat, the mob bursts in, trampling down the women who sought to bar the entrance with their bodies. Several faint, fall to the ground; others flee in panic. The children scream.

Pancracio is about to break the lock of a huge wardrobe when suddenly the doors open and out comes a man with a rifle in his hands.

"Señor Don Mónico!" they all exclaim in surprise.

"Demetrio, please, don't harm me! Please don't harm me! Please don't hurt me! You know, Señor Don Demetrio, I'm your friend!"

Demetrio Macías smiles slyly. "Are friends," he asked, "usually welcomed gun in hand?"

Don Mónico, in consternation, throws himself at Demetrio's feet, clasps his knees, kisses his shoes:

"My wife! . . . My children! . . . Please, Señor Don Demetrio, my friend!"

Demetrio with taut hand puts his gun back in the holster.

A painful silhouette crosses his mind. He sees a woman with a child in her arms walking over the rocks of the sierra in the moonlight. A house in flames. . . .

"Clear out. Everybody outside!" he orders darkly.

His staff obeys. Mónico and the ladies kiss his hands, weeping with gratitude. The mob in the street, talking and laughing, stands waiting for the general's permission to ransack the *cacique's* house.

"I know where they've buried their money but I won't tell," says a youngster with a basket in his hands.

"Hm! I know the right place, mind you," says an old woman carrying a burlap sack to hold whatever the good Lord will provide. "It's on top of something . . . there's a lot of trinkets nearby and then there's a small bag with mother-of-pearl around it. That's the thing to look for!"

"You ain't talking sense, woman," puts in a man. "They ain't such fools as to leave silver lying loose like that. I'm thinking they've got it buried in the well, in a leather bag."

The mob moves slowly; some carry ropes to tie about their bundles, others wooden trays. The women open out their aprons or shawls calculating their capacity. All give thanks to Divine Providence as they wait for their share of the booty.

When Demetrio announces that he will not allow looting and orders them to disband, the mob, disconsolate, obeys him, and soon scatters; but there is a dull rumor among the soldiers and no one moves from his place.

Annoyed, Demetrio repeats this order.

A young man, a recent recruit, his head turned by drink, laughs and walks boldly toward the door. But before he has reached the threshold, a shot lays him low. He falls like a bull pierced in the neck by the matador's sword. Motionless, his smoking gun in his hand, Demetrio waits for the soldiers to withdraw.

"Set fire to the house!" he orders Luis Cervantes when they reach their quarters.

With a curious eagerness Luis Cervantes does not transmit the order but undertakes the task in person.

Two hours later when the city square was black with smoke and enormous tongues of fire rose from Mónico's house, no one could account for the strange behavior of the general.

Chapter 6

They established themselves in a large gloomy house, which likewise belonged to the *cacique* of Moyahua. The previous occupants had already left strong evidences in the patio, which had been converted into a manure pile. The walls, once whitewashed, were now faded and cracked, revealing the bare unbaked adobe; the floor had been torn up by the hoofs of animals; the orchard was littered with rotted branches and dead leaves. From the entrance one stumbled over broken bits of chairs and other furniture covered with dirt.

By ten o'clock, Luis Cervantes yawned with boredom, said good night to Blondie and War Paint, who were downing endless drinks on a bench in the square, and made for the barracks. The drawing room was alone furnished. As he entered, Demetrio, lying on the floor with his eyes wide open, trying to count the beams, gazed at him.

"It's you, eh? What's new? Come on, sit down."

Luis Cervantes first went over to trim the candle, then drew up a chair without a back, a coarse rag doing the duty of a wicker bottom. The legs of the chair squeaked. War Paint's black horse snorted and whirled its crupper in wide circles. Luis Cervantes sank into his seat.

"General, I wish to make my report. Here you have . . ."

"Look here, man, I didn't really want this done, you know. Moyahua is almost like my native town. They'll say this is why we've been fighting!" Demetrio said, looking at the bulging sack of silver Cervantes was passing to him. Cervantes left his seat to squat down by Demetrio's side.

He stretched a blanket over the floor and into it

poured the ten-peso pieces, shining, burning gold.

"First of all, General, only you and I know about this. . . . Secondly, you know well enough that if the sun shines, you should open the window. It's shining in our faces now but what about tomorrow? You should always look ahead. A bullet, a bolting horse, even a wretched cold in the head, and then there are a widow and orphans left in absolute want! . . . The Government? Ha! Ha! . . . Just go see Carranza or Villa or any of the big chiefs and try and tell them about your family. . . . If they answer with a kick you know where, they'll say they're giving you a handful of jewels. And they're right; we did not rise up in arms to make some Carranza or Villa President of our Republic. No—we fought to defend the sacred rights of the people against the tyranny of some vile *cacique*. And so, just as Villa or Carranza aren't going to ask our consent to the payment they're getting for the services they're rendering the country, we for our part don't have to ask anybody's permission about anything either."

Demetrio half stood up, grasped a bottle that stood nearby, drained it, then spat out the liquor, swelling out his cheeks.

"By God, my boy, you've certainly got the gift of gab!"

Luis felt dizzy, faint. The spattered beer seemed to intensify the stench of the refuse on which they sat; a carpet of orange and banana peels, fleshlike slices of watermelon, moldy masses of mangoes and sugar-cane, all mixed up with cornhusks from tamales and human offal.

Demetrio's calloused hands shuffled through the brilliant coins, counting and counting. Recovering from his nausea, Luis Cervantes pulled out a small box of Fallières phosphate and poured forth rings, brooches, pendants, and countless valuable jewels.

"Look here, General, if this mess doesn't blow over

(and it doesn't look as though it would), if the revolution keeps on, there's enough here already for us to live on abroad quite comfortably."

Demetrio shook his head.

"You wouldn't do that!"

"Why not? What are we staying on for? . . . What cause are we defending now?"

"That's something I can't explain, Tenderfoot. But I'm thinking it wouldn't show much guts."

"Take your choice, General," said Luis Cervantes, pointing to the jewels which he had set in a row.

"Oh, you keep it all. . . . Certainly! . . . You know, I don't really care for money at all. I'll tell you the truth! I'm the happiest man in the world, so long as there's always something to drink and a nice little wench that catches my eye. . . ."

"Ha! Ha! You make the funniest jokes, General. Why do you stand for that snake of a War Paint, then?"

"I'll tell you, Tenderfoot, I'm fed up with her. But I'm like that: I just can't tell her so. I'm not brave enough to tell her to go plumb to hell. That's the way I am, see? When I like a woman, I get plain silly; and if she doesn't start something, I've not got the courage to do anything myself." He sighed. "There's Camilla at the ranch for instance. . . . Now, she's not much on looks, I know, but there's a woman I'd like to have. . . ."

"Well, General, we'll go and get her any day you like."

Demetrio winked maliciously.

"I promise you I'll do it."

"Are you sure? Do you really mean it? Look here, if you pull that off for me, I'll give you the watch and chain you're hankering after."

Luis Cervantes' eyes shone. He took the phosphate box, heavy with its contents, and stood up smiling.

"I'll see you tomorrow," he said. "Good night, General! Sleep well."

Chapter 7

"I don't know any more about it than you do. The General told me, 'Quail, saddle your horse and my black mare and follow Cervantes; he's going on an errand for me.' Well, that's what happened. We left here at noon, and reached the ranch early that evening. One-eyed María Antonia took us in. . . . She asked after you, Pancracio. Next morning Luis Cervantes wakes me up. 'Quail, Quail, saddle the horses. Leave me mine but take the General's mare back to Moyahua. I'll catch up after a bit.' The sun was high when he arrived with Camilla. She got off and we stuck her on the General's mare."

"Well, and her? What sort of a face did she make coming back?" one of the men inquired.

"Hum! She was so damned happy she was gabbing all the way."

"And the tenderfoot?"

"Just as quiet as he always is, you know him."

"I think," Venancio expressed his opinion with great seriousness, "that if Camilla woke up in the General's bed, it was just a mistake. We drank a lot, remember! That alcohol went to our heads; we must have lost our senses."

"What the hell do you mean: alcohol! It was all cooked up between Cervantes and the General."

"Certainly! That city dude's nothing but a . . ."

"I don't like to talk about friends behind their backs," said Blondie, "but I can tell you this: one of the two sweethearts he had, one was mine, and the other was for the General."

They burst into guffaws of laughter.

When War Paint realized what had happened, she

sought out Camilla and spoke with great affection:

"Poor little child! Tell me how all this happened."

Camilla's eyes were red from weeping.

"He lied to me! He lied! He came to the ranch and he told me, 'Camilla, I came just to get you. Do you want to go away with me?' You can be sure I wanted to go with him; when it comes to loving, I adore him. Yes, I adore him. Look how thin I've grown just pining away for him. Mornings I used to loathe to grind corn, Mamma would call me to eat, and anything I put in my mouth had no taste at all."

Once more she burst into tears, stuffing the corner of her apron into her mouth to drown her sobs.

"Look here, I'll help you out of this mess. Don't be silly, child, don't cry. Don't think about the dude any more! Honest to God, he's not worth it. You surely know his game, dear? . . . That's the only reason why the General stands for him. What a goose! . . . All right, you want to go back home?"

"The Holy Virgin protect me. My mother would beat me to death!"

"She'll do nothing of the sort. You and I can fix things. Listen! The soldiers are leaving any moment now. When Demetrio tells you to get ready, you tell him you feel pains all over your body as though someone had hit you; then you lie down and start yawning and shivering. Then put your hand on your forehead and say, 'I'm burning up with fever.' I'll tell Demetrio to leave us both here, that I'll stay to take care of you, that as soon as you're feeling all right again, we'll catch up with them. But instead of that, I'll see that you get home safe and sound."

Chapter 8

The sun had set, the town was lost in the drab melancholy of its ancient streets amid the frightened silence of its inhabitants, who had retired very early, when Luis Cervantes reached Primitivo's general store, his arrival interrupting a party that promised great doings.

Demetrio was engaged in getting drunk with his old comrades. The entire space before the bar was occupied. War Paint and Blondie had tied up their horses outside; but the other officers had stormed in brutally, horses and all. Embroidered hats with enormous and concave brims bobbed up and down everywhere. The horses wheeled about, prancing; tossing their restive heads; their fine breed showing in their black eyes, their small ears and dilating nostrils. Over the infernal din of the drunkards, the heavy breathing of the horses, the stamp of their hoofs on the tiled floor, and occasionally a quick, nervous whinny rang out.

A trivial episode was being commented upon when Luis Cervantes came in. A man, dressed in civilian clothes, with a round, black, bloody hole in his forehead, lay stretched out in the middle of the street, his mouth gaping. Opinion was at first divided but finally all concurred with Blondie's sound reasoning. The poor dead devil lying out there was the church sexton. . . . But what an idiot! His own fault, of course! Who in the name of hell could be so foolish as to dress like a city dude, with trousers, coat, cap, and all? Pancracio simply could not bear the sight of a city man in front of him! And that was that!

Eight musicians, playing wind instruments, interrupted their labors at Cervantes' command. Their faces were round and red as suns, their eyes popping, for they had been blowing on their brass instruments since dawn.

"General," Luis said pushing his way through the men on horseback, "a messenger has arrived with orders to proceed immediately to the pursuit and capture of Orozco and his men."

Faces that had been dark and gloomy were now illumined with joy.

"To Jalisco, boys!" cried Blondie, pounding on the counter.

"Make ready, all you darling Jalisco girls of my heart, for I'm coming along too!" Quail shouted, twisting back the brim of his hat.

The enthusiasm and rejoicing were general. Demetrio's friends, in the excitement of drunkenness, offered their services. Demetrio was so happy that he could scarcely speak. They were going to fight Orozco and his men! At last, they would pit themselves against real men! At last they would stop shooting down the Federals like so many rabbits or wild turkeys.

"If I could get hold of Orozco alive," Blondie said, "I'd rip off the soles of his feet and make him walk twenty-four hours over the sierra!"

"Was that the guy who killed Madero?" asked Meco.

"No," Blondie replied solemnly, "but once when I was a waiter at 'El Mónico,' up in Chihuahua, he hit me in the face!"

"Give Camilla the roan mare," Demetrio ordered Pancracio, who was already saddling the horses.

"Camilla can't go!" said War Paint promptly.

"Who in hell asked for your opinion?" Demetrio retorted angrily.

"It's true, isn't it, Camilla? You were sore all over, weren't you? And you've got a fever right now?"

"Well—anything Demetrio says."

"Don't be a fool! say 'No,' come on, say 'No,'"

War Paint whispered nervously into Camilla's ear.

"I'll tell you, War Paint. . . . It's funny, but I'm beginning to fall for him. . . . Would you believe it!" Camilla whispered back.

War Paint turned purple, her cheeks swelled. Without a word she went out to get her horse that Blondie was saddling.

Chapter 9

A whirlwind of dust, scorching down the road, suddenly broke into violent diffuse masses; and Demetrio's army emerged, a chaos of horses, broad chests, tangled manes, dilated nostrils, oval, wide eyes, hoofs flying in the air, legs stiffened from endless galloping; and of men with bronze faces, ivory teeth, and flashing eyes, their rifles in their hands or slung across the saddles.

Demetrio and Camilla brought up the rear. She was still nervous, white-lipped and parched; he was angry at their futile maneuver. For there had been battles, no followers of Orozco's to be seen. A handful of Federals, routed. A poor devil of a priest left dangling from a mesquite; a few dead, scattered over the field, who had once been united under the archaic slogan, RIGHTS AND RELIGION, with, on their breasts, the red cloth insignia: *Halt! The Sacred Heart of Jesus is with me!*

"One good thing about it is that I've collected all my back pay," Quail said, exhibiting some gold watches and rings stolen from the priest's house.

"It's fun fighting this way," Manteca cried, spicing every other word with an oath. "You know why the hell you're risking your hide."

In the same hand with which he held the reins, he clutched a shining ornament that he had torn from one of the holy statues.

After Quail, an expert in such matters, had examined Manteca's treasure covetously, he uttered a solemn guffaw.

"Hell, your ornament is nothing but tin!"

"Why in hell are you hanging on to that poison?"

Pancracio asked Blondie who appeared dragging a prisoner.

"Do you want to know why? Because it's a long time since I've had a good look at a man's face when a rope tightens around his neck!"

The fat prisoner breathed with difficulty as he followed Blondie on foot; his face was sunburnt, his eyes red; his forehead beaded with sweat, his wrists tightly bound together.

"Here, Anastasio, lend me your lasso. Mine's not strong enough; this bird will bust it. No, by God, I've changed my mind, friend Federal: think I'll kill you on the spot, because you are pulling too hard. Look, all the mesquites are still a long way off and there are no telegraph poles to hang you to!"

Blondie pulled his gun out, pressed the muzzle against the prisoner's chest and brought his finger against the trigger slowly . . . slowly. . . . The prisoner turned pale as a corpse; his face lengthened; his eyelids were fixed in a glassy stare. He breathed in agony, his whole body shook as with ague. Blondie kept his gun in the same position for a moment long as all eternity. His eyes shone queerly. An expression of supreme pleasure lit up his fat puffy face.

"No, friend Federal," he drawled, putting back his gun into the holster; "I'm not going to kill you just yet. . . . I'll make you my orderly. You'll see that I'm not so hardhearted!"

Slyly he winked at his companions. The prisoner had turned into an animal; he gulped, panting, dry-mouthed. Camilla, who had witnessed the scene, spurred her horse and caught up with Demetrio.

"What a brute that Blondie is: you ought to see what he did to a wretched prisoner," she said. Then she told Demetrio what had occurred. The latter wrinkled his brow but made no answer.

War Paint called Camilla aside.

"Hey you . . . what are you gabbling about? Blondie's my man, understand? From now on, you know how things are: whatever you've got against him you've got against me too! I'm warning you."

Camilla, frightened, hurried back to Demetrio's side.

Chapter 10

The men camped in a meadow, near three small lone houses standing in a row, their white walls cutting the purple fringe of the horizon. Demetrio and Camilla rode toward them. Inside the corral a man, clad in shirt and trousers of cheap white cloth, sat greedily puffing at a cornhusk cigarette. Another man sitting beside him on a flat cut stone was shelling corn. Kicking the air with one dry, withered leg, the extremity of which was like a goat's hoof, he frightened the chickens away.

"Hurry up, 'Pifanio," said the man who was smoking, "the sun has gone down already and you haven't taken the animals to water."

A horse neighed outside the corral; both men glanced up in amazement. Demetrio and Camilla were looking over the corral wall at them.

"I just want a place to sleep for my woman and me," Demetrio said reassuringly.

As he explained that he was the chief of a small army which was to camp nearby that night, the man smoking, who owned the place, bid them enter with great deference. He ran to fetch a broom and a pail of water to dust and wash the best corner of the hut as decent lodging for his distinguished guests.

"Here, 'Pifanio, go out there and unsaddle the horses."

The man who was shelling corn stood up with an effort. He was clad in a tattered shirt and vest. His torn trousers, split at the seam, looked like the wings of a cold, stricken bird; two strings of cloth dangled from his waist. As he walked, he described grotesque circles.

"Surely you're not fit to do any work!" Demetrio said, refusing to allow him to touch the saddles.

"Poor man," the owner cried from within the hut, "he's lost all his strength. . . . But he surely works for his pay. . . . He starts working the minute God Almighty himself gets up, and it's after sundown now but he's working still!"

Demetrio went out with Camilla for a stroll about the encampment. The meadow, golden, furrowed, stripped even of the smallest bushes, extended limitless in its immense desolation. The three tall ash trees which stood in front of the small house, with dark green crests, round and waving, with rich foliage and branches drooping to the very ground, seemed a veritable miracle.

"I don't know why but I feel there's a lot of sadness around here," said Demetrio.

"Yes," Camilla answered, "I feel that way too."

On the bank of a small stream, 'Pifanio was strenuously tugging at a rope with a large can tied to the end of it. He poured a stream of water over a heap of fresh, cool grass; in the twilight, the water glimmered like crystal. A thin cow, a scrawny nag, and a burro drank noisily together.

Demetrio recognized the limping servant and asked him: "How much do you get a day?"

"Eight cents a day, boss."

He was an insignificant, scrofulous wraith of a man with green eyes and straight, fair hair. He whined complaint of his boss, the ranch, his bad luck, his dog's life.

"You certainly earn your pay all right, my lad," Demetrio interrupted kindly. "You complain and complain, but you aren't no loafer, you work, and work." Then, aside to Camilla: "There's always more damned fools in the valley than among us folk in the sierra, don't you think?"

"Of course!" she replied.

They went on. The valley was lost in darkness; stars

came out. Demetrio put his arm around Camilla's waist amorously and whispered in her ear.

"Yes," she answered in a faint voice.

She was indeed beginning to "fall for him" as she had expressed it.

Demetrio slept badly. He flung out of the house very early.

"Something is going to happen to me," he thought.

It was a silent dawn, with faint murmurs of joy. A thrush sang timidly in one of the ash trees. The animals in the corral trampled on the refuse. The pig grunted its somnolence. The orange tints of the sun streaked the sky; the last star flickered out.

Demetrio walked slowly to the encampment.

He was thinking of his plow, his two black oxen—young beasts they were, who had worked in the fields only two years—of his two acres of well-fertilized corn. The face of his young wife came to his mind, clear and true as life: he saw her strong, soft features, so gracious when she smiled on her husband, so proudly fierce toward strangers. But when he tried to conjure up the image of his son, his efforts were vain; he had forgotten. . . .

He reached the camp. Lying among the furrows, the soldiers slept with the horses, heads bowed, eyes closed.

"Our horses are pretty tired, Anastasio. I think we ought to stay here at least another day."

"Well, Compadre Demetrio, I'm hankering for the sierra. . . . If you only knew. . . . You may not believe me but nothing strikes me right here. I don't know what I miss but I know I miss something. I feel sad . . . lost . . . ."

"How many hours' ride from here to Limón?"

"It's no matter of hours; it's three days' hard riding, Demetrio."

"You know," Demetrio said softly, "I feel as though

I'd like to see my wife again!"

Shortly after, War Paint sought out Camilla.

"That's one on you, my dear. . . . Demetrio's going to leave you flat! He told me so himself; 'I'm going to get my real woman,' he says, and he says, 'Her skin is white and tender . . . and her rosy cheeks. . . . How beautiful she is!' But you don't have to leave him, you know; if you're set on staying, well—they've got a child, you know, and I suppose you could drag it around. . . ."

When Demetrio returned, Camilla, weeping, told him everything.

"Don't pay no attention to that crazy baggage. It's all lies, lies!"

Since Demetrio did not go to Limón or remember his wife again, Camilla grew very happy. War Paint had merely stung herself, like a scorpion. . . .

Chapter 11

Before dawn, they left for Tepatitlán. Their silhouettes wavered indistinctly over the road and the fields that bordered it, rising and falling with the monotonous, rhythmical gait of their horses, then faded away in the nacreous light of the swooning moon that bathed the valley.

Dogs barked in the distance.

"By noon we'll reach Tepatitlán, Cuquío tomorrow, and then . . . on to the sierra!" Demetrio said.

"Don't you think it advisable to go to Aguascalientes first, General?" Luis Cervantes asked.

"What for?"

"Our funds are melting slowly."

"Nonsense . . . forty thousand pesos in eight days!"

"Well, you see, just this week we recruited over five hundred new men; all the money's gone in advance loans and gratuities," Luis Cervantes answered in a low voice.

"No! We'll go straight to the sierra. We'll see later on."

"Yes, to the sierra!" many of the men shouted.

"To the sierra! To the sierra! Hurrah for the mountains!"

The plains seemed to torture them; they spoke with enthusiasm, almost with delirium, of the sierra. They thought of the mountains as of a most desirable mistress long since unvisited.

Dawn broke behind a cloud of fine reddish dust; the sun rose an immense curtain of fiery purple. Luis Cervantes pulled his reins and waited for Quail.

"What's the last word on our deal, Quail?"

"I told you, Tenderfoot: two hundred for the watch alone."

"No! I'll buy the lot: watches, rings, everything else. How much?"

Quail hesitated, turned slightly pale; then he cried spiritedly:

"Two thousand in bills, for the whole business!"

Luis Cervantes gave himself away. His eyes shone with such an obvious greed that Quail recanted and said:

"Oh, I was just fooling you. I won't sell nothing! Just the watch, see? And that's only because I owe Pancracio two hundred. He beat me at cards last night!"

Luis Cervantes pulled out four crisp "double-face" bills of Villa's issue and placed them in Quail's hands.

"I'd like to buy the lot. . . . Besides, nobody will offer you more than that!"

As the sun began to beat down upon them, Manteca suddenly shouted:

"Ho, Blondie, your orderly says he doesn't care to go on living. He says he's too damned tired to walk."

The prisoner had fallen in the middle of the road, utterly exhausted.

"Well, well!" Blondie shouted, retracing his steps. "So little mama's boy is tired, eh? Poor little fellow. I'll buy a glass case and keep you in a corner of my house just as if you were the Virgin Mary's own little son. You've got to reach home first, see? So I'll help you a little, sonny!"

He drew his sword out and struck the prisoner several times.

"Let's have a look at your rope, Pancracio," he said. There was a strange gleam in his eyes. Quail observed that the prisoner no longer moved arm or leg. Blondie burst into a loud guffaw: "The Goddamned fool. Just as I was learning him to do without food, too!"

"Well, mate, we're almost to Guadalajara," Venancio said, glancing over the smiling row of houses in Tepatitlán nestling against the hillside.

They entered joyously. From every window rosy cheeks, dark luminous eyes observed them. The schools were quickly converted into barracks; Demetrio found lodging in the chapel of an abandoned church.

The soldiers scattered about as usual pretending to seek arms and horses, but in reality for the sole purpose of looting.

In the afternoon some of Demetrio's men lay stretched out on the church steps, scratching their bellies. Venancio, his chest and shoulders bare, was gravely occupied in killing the fleas in his shirt. A man drew near the wall and sought permission to speak to the commander. The soldiers raised their heads; but no one answered.

"I'm a widower, gentlemen. I've got nine children and I barely make a living with the sweat of my brow. Don't be hard on a poor widower!"

"Don't you worry about women, Uncle," said Meco, who was rubbing his feet with tallow, "we've got War Paint here with us; you can have her for nothin'."

The man smiled bitterly.

"She's only got one fault," Pancracio observed, stretched out on the ground, staring at the blue sky, "she goes mad over any man she sees."

They laughed loudly; but Venancio with utmost gravity pointed to the chapel door. The stranger entered timidly and confided his troubles to Demetrio. The soldiers had cleaned him out; they had not left a single grain of corn.

"Why did you let them?" Demetrio asked indolently.

The man persisted, lamenting and weeping. Luis Cervantes was about to throw him out with an insult. But Camilla intervened.

"Come on, Demetrio, don't be harsh, give him an order to get his corn back."

Luis Cervantes was obliged to obey; he scrawled a few lines to which Demetrio appended an illegible scratch.

"May God repay you, my child! God will lead you to heaven that you may enjoy his glory. Ten bushels of corn are barely enough for this year's food!" the man cried, weeping for gratitude. Then he took the paper, kissed everybody's hand, and withdrew.

Chapter 12

They had almost reached Cuquío, when Anastasio Montáñez rode up to Demetrio: "Listen, Compadre, I almost forgot to tell you. . . . You ought to have seen the wonderful joke that man Blondie played. You know what he did with the old man who came to complain about the corn we'd taken away for horses? Well, the old man took the paper and went to the barracks. 'Right you are, brother, come in,' said Blondie, 'come in, come in here; to give you back what's yours is only the right thing to do. How many bushels did we steal? Ten? Sure it wasn't more than ten? . . . That's right, about fifteen, eh? Or was it twenty, perhaps? . . . Try and remember, friend. . . . Of course you're a poor man, aren't you, and you've a lot of kids to raise. . . . Yes, twenty it was. All right, now! It's not ten or fifteen or twenty I'm going to give you. You're going to count for yourself. . . . One, two, three . . . and when you've had enough you just tell me and I'll stop.' And Blondie pulled out his sword and beat him till he cried for mercy."

War Paint rocked in her saddle, convulsed with mirth. Camilla, unable to control herself, blurted out:

"The beast! His heart's rotten to the core! No wonder I loathe him!"

At once War Paint's expression changed.

"What the hell is it to you!" she scowled. Camilla, frightened, spurred her horse forward. War Paint did likewise and, as she trotted past Camilla, suddenly she reached out, seized the other's hair and pulled with all her might. Camilla's horse shied; Camilla, trying to brush her hair back from over her eyes, abandoned the reins. She hesitated, lost her balance and fell in the road, striking her forehead against the stones.

War Paint, weeping with laughter, pressed on with utmost skill and caught Camilla's horse. "Come on, Tenderfoot; here's a job for you," Pancracio said as he saw Camilla on Demetrio's saddle, her face covered with blood.

Luis Cervantes hurried toward her with some cotton; but Camilla, choking down her sobs and wiping her eyes, said hoarsely:

"Not from you! If I was dying, I wouldn't accept anything from you . . . not even water."

In Cuquío Demetrio received a message.

"We've got to go back to Tepatitlán, General," said Luis Cervantes, scanning the dispatch rapidly. "You've got to leave the men there while you go to Lagos and take the train over to Aguascalientes."

There was much heated protest, the men muttering to themselves or even groaning out loud. Some of them, mountaineers, swore that they would not continue with the troop.

Camilla wept all night. On the morrow at dawn, she begged Demetrio to let her return home.

"If you don't like me, all right," he answered sullenly.

"That's not the reason. I care for you a lot, really. But you know how it is. That woman . . ."

"Never mind about her. It's all right! I'll send her off to hell today. I had already decided that."

Camilla dried her tears. . . .

Every horse was saddled; the men were waiting only for orders from the Chief. Demetrio went up to War Paint and said under his breath:

"You're not coming with us."

"What!" she gasped.

"You're going to stay here or go wherever you damn well please, but you're not coming along with us."

"What? What's that you're saying?" Still she could not catch Demetrio's meaning. Then the truth dawned upon her. "You want to send me away? By God, I suppose you believe all the filth that bitch . . ."

And War Paint proceeded to insult Camilla, Luis Cervantes, Demetrio, and anyone she happened to remember at the moment, with such power and originality that the soldiers listened in wonder to vituperation that transcended their wildest dream of profanity and filth.

Demetrio waited a long time patiently. Then, as she showed no sign of stopping, he said to a soldier quite calmly:

"Throw this drunken woman out."

"Blondie, Blondie, love of my life! Help! Come and show them you're a real man! Show them they're nothing but sons of bitches! . . ."

She gesticulated, kicked, and shouted.

Blondie appeared; he had just got up. His blue eyes blinked under heavy lids; his voice rang hoarse. He asked what had occurred; someone explained. Then he went up to War Paint, and with great seriousness, said:

"Yes? Really? Well, if you want my opinion, I think this is just what ought to happen. So far as I'm concerned, you can go straight to hell. We're all fed up with you, see?"

War Paint's face turned to granite; she tried to speak but her muscles were rigid.

The soldiers laughed. Camilla, terrified, held her breath.

War Paint stared slowly at everyone about her. It all took no more than a few seconds. In a trice she bent down, drew a sharp, gleaming dagger from her stocking and leapt at Camilla.

A shrill cry. A body fell, the blood spurting from it.

"Kill her, Goddamn it," cried Demetrio, beyond himself. "Kill her!"

Two soldiers fell upon War Paint, but she brandished her dagger, defying them to touch her:

"Not the likes of you, Goddamn you! Kill me yourself, Demetrio!"

War Paint stepped forward, surrendered her dagger and, thrusting her breast forward, let her arms fall to her side.

Demetrio picked up the dagger, red with blood, but his eyes clouded; he hesitated, took a step backward. Then, with a heavy hoarse voice he growled, enraged:

"Get out of here! Quick!"

No one dared stop her. She moved off slowly, mute, somber.

Blondie's shrill, guttural voice broke the silent stupor:

"Thank God! At last I'm rid of that damned louse!"

Chapter 13

Someone plunged a knife
Deep in my side.
Did he know why?
I don't know why.
Maybe he knew,
I never knew.
The blood flowed out
Of that mortal wound.
Did he know why?
I don't know why.
Maybe he knew,
I never knew.

His head lowered, his hands crossed over the pommel of his saddle, Demetrio in melancholy accents sang the strains of the intriguing song. Then he fell silent; for quite a while he continued to feel oppressed and sad.

"You'll see, as soon as we reach Lagos you'll come out of it, General. There's plenty of pretty girls to give us a good time," Blondie said.

"Right now I feel like getting damn drunk," Demetrio answered, spurring his horse forward and leaving them as if he wished to abandon himself entirely to his sadness.

After many hours of riding he called Cervantes.

"Listen, Tenderfoot, why in hell do we have to go to Aguascalientes?"

"You have to vote for the Provisional President of the Republic, General!"

"President, what? Who in the devil, then, is this man Carranza? I'll be damned if I know what it's all about."

At last they reached Lagos. Blondie bet that he would make Demetrio laugh that evening.

Trailing his spurs noisily over the pavement, Demetrio entered "El Cosmopolita" with Luis Cervantes, Blondie, and his assistants.

The civilians, surprised in their attempt to escape, remained where they were. Some feigned to return to their tables to continue drinking and talking; others hesitantly stepped up to present their respects to the commander.

"General, so pleased! . . . Major! Delighted to meet you!"

"That's right! I love refined and educated friends," Blondie said. "Come on, boys," he added, jovially drawing his gun, "I'm going to play a tune that'll make you all dance."

A bullet ricocheted on the cement floor passing between the legs of the tables, and the smartly dressed young men-about-town began to jump much as a woman jumps when frightened by a mouse under her skirt. Pale as ghosts, they conjured up wan smiles of obsequious approval. Demetrio barely parted his lips, but his followers doubled over with laughter.

"Look, Blondie," Quail shouted, "look at that man going out there. Look, he's limping."

"I guess the bee stung him all right."

Blondie, without turning to look at the wounded man, announced with enthusiasm that he could shoot off the top of a tequila bottle at thirty paces without aiming.

"Come on, friend, stand up," he said to the waiter. He dragged him out by the hand to the patio of the hotel and set a tequila bottle on his head. The poor devil refused. Insane with fright, he sought to escape, but Blondie pulled his gun and took aim.

"Come on, you son of a sea cook! If you keep on I'll give you a nice warm one!"

Blondie went to the opposite wall, raised his gun and fired. The bottle broke into bits, the alcohol poured over the lad's ghastly face."Now it's a go," cried Blondie, running to the bar to get another bottle, which he placed on the lad's head.

He returned to his former position, he whirled about, and shot without aiming. But he hit the waiter's ear instead of the bottle. Holding his sides with laughter, he said to the young waiter:

"Here, kid, take these bills. It ain't much. But you'll be all right with some alcohol and arnica."

After drinking a great deal of alcohol and beer, Demetrio spoke:

"Pay the bill, Blondie, I'm going to leave you."

"I ain't got a penny, General, but that's all right. I'll fix it. How much do we owe you, friend?"

"One hundred and eighty pesos, Chief," the bartender answered amiably.

Quickly, Blondie jumped behind the bar and with a sweep of both arms, knocked down all the glasses and bottles.

"Send the bill to General Villa, understand?"

He left, laughing loudly at his prank.

"Say there, you, where do the girls hang out?" Blondie asked, reeling up drunkenly toward a small well-dressed man, standing at the door of a tailor shop.

The man stepped down to the sidewalk politely to let Blondie pass.

Blondie stopped and looked at him curiously, impertinently.

"Little boy, you're very small and dainty, ain't you? . . . No? . . . Then I'm a liar! . . . That's right! . . . You know the puppet dance. . . . You don't? The hell you don't! . . . I met you in a circus! I know you can even dance on a tightrope! . . . You watch!"

Blondie drew his gun out and began to shoot,

aiming at the tailor's feet; the tailor gave a little jump at every pull of the trigger.

"See! You do know how to dance on the tightrope, don't you?"

Taking his friends by the arm, he ordered them to lead him to the red-light district, punctuating every step by a shot which smashed a street light, or struck some wall, a door, or a distant house.

Demetrio left him and returned to the hotel, singing to himself:

"Someone plunged a knife
Deep in my side.
Did he know why?
I don't know why.
Maybe he knew,
I never knew."

Chapter 14

Stale cigarette smoke, the acrid odors of sweaty clothing, the vapors of alcohol, the breathing of a crowded multitude, worse by far than a trainful of pigs.

Texas hats, adorned with gold braid, and khaki predominate. "Gentlemen, a well-dressed man stole my suitcase in the station. My life's savings! I haven't enough to feed my little boy now!"

The shrill voice, rising to a shriek or trailing off into a sob, is drowned out by the tumult within the train.

"What the hell is the old woman talking about?" Blondie asks, entering in search of a seat.

"Something about a suitcase . . . and a well-dressed man," Pancracio replies. He has already the laps of two civilians to sit on.

Demetrio and the others elbow their way in. Since those on whom Pancracio had sat preferred to stand up, Demetrio and Luis Cervantes quickly seize the vacant seats.

Suddenly a woman who has stood up holding a child all the way from Irapuato, faints. A civilian takes the child in his arms. The others pretend to have seen nothing. Some women, traveling with the soldiers, occupy two or three seats with baggage, dogs, cats, parrots. Some of the men wearing Texan hats laugh at the plump arms and pendulous breasts of the woman who fainted.

"Gentlemen, a well-dressed man stole my suitcase at the station in Silao! All my life's savings . . . I haven't got enough to feed my little boy now! . . ."

The old woman speaks rapidly, parrotlike, sighing and sobbing. Her sharp eyes peer about on all sides. Here she gets a bill, and further on, another. They shower money upon her. She finishes the collection, and goes a few seats ahead.

"Gentlemen, a well-dressed man stole my suitcase in the station at Silao." Her words produce an immediate and certain effect.

A well-dressed man, a dude, a tenderfoot, stealing a suitcase! Amazing, phenomenal! It awakens a feeling of universal indignation. It's a pity: if this well-dressed man were here every one of the generals would shoot him, one after the other!

"There's nothing as vile as a city dude who steals!" a man says, exploding with indignation.

"To rob a poor old lady!"

"To steal from a poor defenseless woman!"

They prove their compassion by word and deed: a harsh verdict against the culprit; a five-peso bill for the victim.

"And I'm telling you the truth," Blondie declares. "Don't think it's wrong to kill, because when you kill, it's always out of anger. But stealing—Bah!"

This profound piece of reasoning meets with unanimous assent. After a short silence while he meditates, a colonel ventures his opinion:

"Everything is all right according to something, see? That is, everything has its circumstances, see? God's own truth is this: I have stolen, and if I say that everyone here has done the trick, I'm not telling a lie, I reckon!"

"Hell, I stole a lot of them sewing machines in Mexico," exclaims a major. "I made more'n five hundred pesos even though I sold them at fifty cents apiece!"

A toothless captain, with hair prematurely white, announces:

"I stole some horses in Zacatecas, all damn fine horses they was, and then I says to myself, 'This is your own little lottery, Pascual Mata,' I says. 'You won't have a worry in all your life after this.' And the damned thing about it was that General Limón took a fancy to the horses too, and he stole them from me!"

"Of course—there's no use denying it, I've stolen too," Blondie confesses. "But ask any one of my partners how much profit I've got. I'm a big spender and my purse is my friends' to have a good time on! I have a better time if I drink myself senseless than I would have sending money back home to the old woman!"

The subject of "I stole," though apparently in-exhaustible, ceases to hold the men's attention. Decks of cards gradually appear on the seats, drawing generals and officers as the light draws mosquitoes.

The excitement of gambling soon absorbs every interest, the heat grows more and more intense. To breathe is to inhale the air of barracks, prison, brothel, and pigsty all in one.

And rising above the babble, from the car ahead ever the shrill voice, "Gentlemen, a well-dressed young man stole . . ."

The streets in Aguascalientes were so many refuse piles. Men in khaki moved to and fro like bees before their hive, overrunning the restaurants, the crapulous lunch houses, the parlous hotels, and the stands of the street vendors on which rotten pork lay alongside grimy cheese.

The smell of these viands whetted the appetites of Demetrio and his men. They forced their way into a small inn, where a disheveled old hag served, on earthenware plates, some pork with bones swimming in a clear chili stew and three tough burnt tortillas. They paid two pesos apiece; as they left Pancracio assured his comrades he was hungrier than when he entered.

"Now," said Demetrio, "we'll go and consult with General Natera!"

They made for the northern leader's billet.

A noisy, excited crowd stopped them at a street crossing. A man, lost in the multitude, was mouthing words in the monotonous, unctuous tones of a prayer. They came up close enough to see him distinctly; he wore a shirt and trousers of cheap white cloth and was repeating:

"All good Catholics should read this prayer to Christ Our Lord upon the Cross with due devotion. Thus they will be immune from storms and pestilence, famine, and war."

"This man's no fool," said Demetrio smiling.

The man waved a sheaf of printed handbills in his hand and cried:

"A quarter of a peso is all you have to pay for this prayer to Christ Our Lord upon the Cross. A quarter . . ."

Then he would duck for a moment, to reappear with a snake's tooth, a sea star, or the skeleton of a fish. In the same predicant tone, he lauded the medical virtues and the mystical powers of every article he sold.

Quail, who had no faith in Venancio, requested the man to pull a tooth out. Blondie purchased a black seed from a certain fruit which protected the possessor from lightning or any other catastrophe. Anastasio Montáñez purchased a prayer to Christ Our Lord upon the Cross, and, folding it carefully, stuck it into his shirt with a pious gesture.

"As sure as there's a God in heaven," Natera said, "this mess hasn't blown over yet. Now it's Villa fighting Carranza."

Without answering him, his eyes fixed in a stare, Demetrio demanded a further explanation.

"It means," Natera said, "that the Convention won't recognize Carranza as First Chief of the Constitutionalist Army. It's going to elect a Provisional

President of the Republic. Do you understand me, General?"

Demetrio nodded assent.

"What's your opinion, General?" asked Natera.

Demetrio shrugged his shoulders:

"It seems to me that the meat of the matter is that we've got to go on fighting, eh? All right! Let's go to it! I'm game to the end, you know."

"Good, but on what side?"

Demetrio, nonplussed, scratched his head:

"Look here, don't ask me any more questions. I never went to school, you know. . . . You gave me the eagle I wear on my hat, didn't you? All right then; you just tell me: 'Demetrio, do this or do that,' and that's all there's to it!"

Part Three

"*Villa? Obregón? Carranza? What's the difference? I love the revolution like a volcano in eruption; I love the volcano, because it's a volcano, the revolution, because it's the revolution!*"

Chapter 1

El Paso, Texas, May 16, 1915

My Dear Venancio:

Due to the pressure of professional duties I have been unable to answer your letter of January 4 before now. As you already know, I was graduated last December. I was sorry to hear of Pancracio's and Manteca's fate, though I am not surprised that they stabbed each other over the gambling table. It is a pity; they were both brave men. I am deeply grieved not to be able to tell Blondie how sincerely and heartily I congratulate him for the only noble and beautiful thing he ever did in his whole life: to have shot himself!

Dear Venancio, although you may have enough money to purchase a degree, I am afraid you won't find it very easy to become a doctor in this country. You know I like you very much, Venancio; and I think you deserve a better fate. But I have an idea which may prove profitable to both of us and which may improve your social position, as you desire. We could do a fine business here if we were to go in as partners and set up a typical Mexican restaurant in this town. I have no reserve funds at the moment since I've spent all I had in getting my college degree, but I have something much more valuable than money; my perfect knowledge of this town and its needs. You can appear as the owner; we will make a monthly division of profits. Besides, concerning a question that interests us both very much, namely, your social improvement, it occurs to me that you play the guitar quite well. In view of the recommendations I could give you and in view of your training as well, you might easily be admitted as a member of some fraternal order; there are several here which would bring you no inconsiderable social prestige.

Don't hesitate, Venancio, come at once and bring your funds. I promise you we'll get rich in no time. My best wishes to the General, to Anastasio, and the rest of the boys.

Your affectionate friend,
Luis Cervantes

Venancio finished reading the letter for the hundredth time and, sighing, repeated:

"Tenderfoot certainly knows how to pull the strings all right!"

"What I can't get into my head," observed Anastasio Montáñez, "is why we keep on fighting. Didn't we finish off this man Huerta and his Federation?"

Neither the General nor Venancio answered; but the same thought kept beating down on their dull brains like a hammer on an anvil.

They ascended the steep hill, their heads bowed, pensive, their horses walking at a slow gait. Stubbornly restless, Anastasio made the same observation to other groups; the soldiers laughed at his candor. If a man has a rifle in his hands and a beltful of cartridges, surely he should use them. That means fighting. Against whom? For whom? That is scarcely a matter of importance.

The endless wavering column of dust moved up the trail, a swirling ant heap of broad straw sombreros, dirty khaki, faded blankets, and black horses. . . .

Not a man but was dying of thirst; no pool or stream or well anywhere along the road. A wave of dust rose from the white, wild sides of a small canyon, swayed mistily on the hoary crest of *huizache* trees and the greenish stumps of cactus. Like a jest, the flowers in the cactus opened out, fresh, solid, aflame, some thorny, others diaphanous.

At noon they reached a hut, clinging to the precipitous sierra, then three more huts strewn over the margin of a river of burnt sand. Everything was silent, desolate. As soon as they saw men on horseback, the people in the huts scurried into the hills to hide. Demetrio grew indignant.

"Bring me anyone you find hiding or running away," he commanded in a loud voice.

"What? What did you say?" Valderrama cried in surprise. "The men of the sierra? Those brave men who've not yet done what those chickens down in Aguascalientes and Zacatecas have done all the time? Our own brothers, who weather storms, who cling to the rocks like moss itself? I protest, sir; I protest!"

He spurred his miserable horse forward and caught up with the General.

"The mountaineers," he said solemnly and emphatically, "are flesh of our flesh, bone of our bone. *Os ex osibus meis et caro de carne mea.* Mountaineers are made from the same timber we're made of! Of the same sound timber from which heroes . . ."

With a confidence as sudden as it was courageous, he hit the General across the chest. The General smiled benevolently.

Valderrama, the tramp, the crazy maker of verses, did he ever know what he said?

When the soldiers reached a small ranch, despairingly, they searched the empty huts and small houses without finding a single stale tortilla, a solitary rotten pepper, or one pinch of salt with which to flavor the horrible taste of dry meat. The owners of the huts, their peaceful brethren, were impassive with the stonelike impassivity of Aztec idols; others, more human, with a slow smile on their colorless lips and beardless faces, watched these fierce men who less than a month ago had made the miserable huts of others tremble with fear, now in their turn fleeing their own huts where the ovens were cold and the water tanks dry, fleeing with their tails between their legs, cringing, like curs kicked out of their own houses.

But the General did not countermand his order. Some soldiers brought back four fugitives, captive and bound.

Chapter 2

"Why do you hide?" Demetrio asked the prisoners.

"We're not hiding, Chief, we're hitting the trail."

"Where to?"

"To our own homes, in God's name, to Durango."

"Is this the road to Durango?"

"Peaceful people can't travel over the main road nowadays, you know that, Chief."

"You're not peaceful people, you're deserters. Where do you come from?" Demetrio said, eyeing them with keen scrutiny.

The prisoners grew confused; they looked at each other hesitatingly, unable to give a prompt answer.

"They're Carranzistas," one of the soldiers said.

"Carranzistas hell!" one of them said proudly. "I'd rather be a pig."

"The truth is we're deserters," another said. "After the defeat we deserted from General Villa's troops this side of Celaya."

"General Villa defeated? Ha! Ha! That's a good joke."

The soldiers laughed. But Demetrio's brow was wrinkled as though a black shadow had passed over his eyes.

"There ain't a son of a bitch on earth who can beat General Villa!" said a bronzed veteran with a scar clear across the face.

Without a change of expression, one of the deserters stared persistently at him and said:

"I know who you are. When we took Torreón you were with General Urbina. In Zacatecas you were with General Natera and then you shifted to the Jalisco troops. Am I lying?"

These words met with a sudden and definite effect. The prisoners gave a detailed account of the tremendous defeat of Villa at Celaya. Demetrio's men listened in silence, stupefied.

Before resuming their march, they built a fire on which to roast some bull meat. Anastasio Montáñez, searching for food among the *huizache* trees, descried the close-cropped neck of Valderrama's horse in the distance among the rocks.

"Hey! Come here, you fool, after all there ain't been no gravy!" he shouted.

Whenever anything was said about shooting someone, Valderrama, the romantic poet, would disappear for a whole day.

Hearing Anastasio's voice, Valderrama was convinced that the prisoners had been set at liberty. A few moments later, he was joined by Venancio and Demetrio.

"Heard the news?" Venancio asked gravely.

"No."

"It's very serious. A terrible mess! Villa was beaten at Celaya by Obregón and Carranza is winning all along the line! We're done for!"

Valderrama's gesture was disdainful and solemn as an emperor's. "Villa? Obregón? Carranza? What's the difference? I love the revolution like a volcano in eruption; I love the volcano because it's a volcano, the revolution because it's the revolution! What do I care about the stones left above or below after the cataclysm? What are they to me?"

In the glare of the midday sun the reflection of a white tequila bottle glittered on his forehead; and, jubilant, he ran toward the bearer of such a marvelous gift.

"I like this crazy fool," Demetrio said with a smile. "He says things sometimes that make you think."

They resumed their march; their uncertainty

translated into a lugubrious silence. Slowly, inevitably, the catastrophe must come; it was even now being realized. Villa defeated was a fallen god; when gods cease to be omnipotent, they are nothing.

Quail spoke. His words faithfully interpreted the general opinion:

"What the hell, boys! Every spider's got to spin his own web now!"

Chapter 3

In Zacatecas and Aguascalientes, in the little country towns and the neighboring communities, haciendas and ranches were deserted. When one of the officers found a barrel of tequila, the event assumed miraculous proportions. Everything was conducted with secrecy and care; deep mystery was preserved to oblige the soliders to leave on the morrow before sunrise under Anastasio and Venancio. When Demetrio awoke to the strains of music, his general staff, now composed chiefly of young ex-government officers, told him of the discovery, and Quail, interpreting the thoughts of his colleagues, said sententiously:

"These are bad times and you've got to take advantage of everythin'. If there are some days when a duck can swim, there's others when he can't take a drink."

The string musicians played all day; the most solemn honors were paid to the barrel: but Demetrio was very sad.

> *"Did he know why?*
> *I don't know why."*

He kept repeating the same refrain.

In the afternoon there were cockfights. Demetrio sat down with the chief officers under the roof of the municipal portals in front of a city square covered with weeds, a tumbled kiosk, and some abandoned adobe houses.

"Valderrama," Demetrio called, looking away from the ring with tired eyes, "come and sing me a song—sing 'The Undertaker.'"

But Valderrama did not hear him; he had no eyes

for the fight; he was reciting an impassioned soliloquy as he watched the sunset over the hills.

With solemn gestures and emphatic tones, he said:

"O Lord, Lord, pleasurable it is this thy land! I shall build me three tents: one for Thee, one for Moses, one for Elijah!"

"Valderrama," Demetrio shouted again. "Come and sing 'The Undertaker' song for me."

"Hey, crazy, the General is calling you," an officer shouted.

Valderrama with his eternally complacent smile went over to Demetrio's seat and asked the musicians for a guitar.

"Silence," the gamesters cried. Valderrama finished tuning his instrument.

Quail and Meco let loose on the sand a pair of cocks armed with long sharp blades attached to their legs. One was light red; his feathers shone with beautiful obsidian glints. The other was sand-colored with feathers like scales burned slowly to a fiery copper color.

The fight was swift and fierce as a duel between men. As though moved by springs, the roosters flew at each other. Their feathers stood up on their arched necks; their combs were erect, their legs taut. For an instant they swung in the air without even touching the ground, their feathers, beaks, and claws lost in a dizzy whirlwind. The red rooster suddenly broke, tossed with his legs to heaven outside the chalk lines. His vermilion eyes closed slowly, revealing eyelids of pink coral; his tangled feathers quivered and shook convulsively amid a pool of blood.

Valderrama, who could not repress a gesture of violent indignation, began to play. With the first melancholy strains of the tune, his anger disappeared. His eyes gleamed with the light of madness. His glance strayed over the square, the tumbled kiosk, the old adobe houses, over the mountains in the background, and over the sky, burning like a roof afire. He began to sing. He put such feeling into his voice and such expression into the strings that, as he finished, Demetrio turned his head aside to hide his tears.

But Valderrama fell upon him, embraced him warmly, and with a familiarity he showed everyone at the appropriate moment, he whispered:

"Drink them! . . . Those are beautiful tears."

Demetrio asked for the bottle, passed it to Valderrama. Greedily the poet drank half its contents in one gulp; then, showing only the whites of his eyes, he faced the spectators dramatically and, in a highly theatrical voice, cried:

"Here you may witness the blessings of the revolution caught in a single tear."

Then he continued to talk like a madman, but like a madman whose vast prophetic madness encompassed all about him, the dusty weeds, the tumbled kiosk, the gray houses, the lovely hills, and the immeasurable sky.

Chapter 4

Juchipila rose in the distance, white, bathed in sunlight, shining in the midst of a thick forest at the foot of a proud, lofty mountain, pleated like a turban.

Some of the soldiers, gazing at the spire of the church, sighed sadly. They marched forward through the canyon, uncertain, unsteady, as blind men walking without a hand to guide them. The bitterness of the exodus pervaded them.

"Is that town Juchipila?" Valderrama asked.

In the first stage of his drunkenness, Valderrama had been counting the crosses scattered along the road, along the trails, in the hollows near the rocks, in the tortuous paths, and along the riverbanks. Crosses of black timber newly varnished, makeshift crosses built out of two logs, crosses of stones piled up and plastered together, crosses whitewashed on crumbling walls, humble crosses drawn with charcoal on the surface of whitish rocks. The traces of the first blood shed by the revolutionists of 1910, murdered by the Government.

Before Juchipila was lost from sight, Valderrama got off his horse, bent down, kneeled, and gravely kissed the ground.

The soldiers passed by without stopping. Some laughed at the crazy man, others jested. Valderrama, deaf to all about him, breathed his unctuous prayer:

"O Juchipila, cradle of the Revolution of 1910, O blessed land, land steeped in the blood of martyrs, blood of dreamers, the only true men . . ."

"Because they had no time to be bad!" an ex-Federal officer interjected as he rode.

Interrupting his prayer, Valderrama frowned, burst

into stentorian laughter, reechoed by the rocks, and ran toward the officer begging for a swallow of tequila.

Soldiers minus an arm or leg, cripples, rheumatics, and consumptives spoke bitterly of Demetrio. Young whippersnappers were given officers' commissions and wore stripes on their hats without a day's service, even before they knew how to handle a rifle, while the veterans, exhausted in a hundred battles, now incapacitated for work, the veterans who had set out as simple privates, were still simple privates. The few remaining officers among Demetrio's friends also grumbled, because his staff was made up of wealthy, dapper young men who oiled their hair and used perfume.

"The worst part of it," Venancio said, "is that we're gettin' overcrowded with Federals!"

Anastasio himself, who invariably found only praise for Demetrio's conduct, now seemed to share the general discontent.

"See here, brothers," he said, "I spits out the truth when I sees something. I always tell the boss that if these people stick to us very long we'll be in a hell of a fix. Certainly! How can anyone think otherwise? I've no hair on my tongue; and by the mother that bore me, I'm going to tell Demetrio so myself."

Demetrio listened benevolently, and, when Anastasio had finished, he replied:

"You're right, there's no gettin' around it, we're in a bad way. The soldiers grumble about the officers, the officers grumble about us, see? And we're damn well ready now to send both Villa and Carranza to hell to have a good time all by themselves. . . . I guess we're in the same fix as that peon from Tepatitlán who complained about his boss all day long but worked on just the same. That's us. We kick and kick, but we keep on killing and killing. But there's no use in saying anything to them!"

"Why, Demetrio?"

"Hm, I don't know. . . . Because . . . because . . . do you see? . . . What we've got to do is to make the men toe the mark. I've got orders to stop a band of men coming through Cuquío, see? In a few days we'll have to fight the Carranzistas. It will be great to beat the hell out of them."

Valderrama, the tramp, who had enlisted in Demetrio's army one day without anyone remembering the time or the place, overheard some of Demetrio's words. Fools do not eat fire. That very day Valderrama disappeared mysteriously as he had come.

Chapter 5

They entered the streets of Juchipila as the church bells rang, loud and joyfully, with that peculiar tone that thrills every mountaineer.

"It makes me think we are back in the days when the revolution was just beginning, when the bells rang like mad in every town we entered and everybody came out with music, flags, cheers, and fireworks to welcome us," said Anastasio Montáñez.

"They don't like us no more," Demetrio returned.

"Of course. We're crawling back like a dog with its tail between its legs," Quail remarked.

"It ain't that, I guess. They don't give a whoop for the other side either."

"But why should they like us?"

They spoke no more.

Presently they reached the city square and stopped in front of an octagonal, rough, massive church, reminiscent of the colonial period. At one time the square must have been a garden, judging from the bare stunted orange trees planted between iron and wooden benches. The sonorous, joyful bells rang again. From within the church, the honeyed voices of a female chorus rose melancholy and grave. To the strains of a guitar, the young girls of the town sang the "Mysteries."

"What's the fiesta, lady?" Venancio asked of an old woman who was running toward the church.

"The Sacred Heart of Jesus!" answered the pious woman, panting.

They remembered that one year ago they had captured Zacatecas. They grew sadder still.

Juchipila, like the other towns they had passed

through on their way from Tepic, by way of Jalisco, Aguascalientes and Zacatecas, was in ruins. The black trail of the incendiaries showed in the roofless houses, in the burnt arcades. Almost all the houses were closed, yet, here and there, those still open offered, in ironic contrast, portals gaunt and bare as the white skeletons of horses scattered over the roads. The terrible pangs of hunger seemed to speak from every face; hunger on every dusty cheek, in their dusty countenances; in the hectic flame of their eyes, which, when they met a soldier, blazed with hatred. In vain the soldiers scoured the streets in search of food, biting their lips in anger. A single lunchroom was open; at once they filled it. No beans, no tortillas, only chili and tomato sauce. In vain the officers showed their pocketbooks stuffed with bills or used threats:

"Yea, you've got papers all right! That's all you've brought! Try and eat them, will you?" said the owner, an insolent old shrew with an enormous scar on her cheek, who told them she had already lain with a dead man, "to cure her from ever feeling frightened again."

Despite the melancholy and desolation of the town, while the women sang in the church, birds sang in the foliage, and the thrushes piped their lyrical strain on the withered branches of the orange trees.

Chapter 6

Demetrio Macias' wife, mad with joy, rushed along the trail to meet him, leading a child by the hand.

An absence of almost two years!

They embraced each other and stood speechless. She wept, sobbed. Demetrio stared in astonishment at his wife who seemed to have aged ten or twenty years. Then he looked at the child who gazed up at him in surprise. His heart leaped to his mouth as he saw in the child's features his own steel features and fiery eyes exactly reproduced. He wanted to hold him in his arms, but the frightened child took refuge in his mother's skirts.

"It's your own father, baby! It's your daddy!"

The child hid his face within the folds of his mother's skirt, still hostile.

Demetrio handed the reins of his horse to his orderly and walked slowly along the steep trail with his wife and son.

"Blessed be the Virgin Mary, Praise be to God! Now you'll never leave us any more, will you? Never . . . never. . . . You'll stay with us always?"

Demetrio's face grew dark. Both remained silent, lost in anguish. Demetrio suppressed a sigh. Memories crowded and buzzed through his brain like bees about a hive.

A black cloud rose behind the sierra and a deafening roar of thunder resounded. The rain began to fall in heavy drops; they sought refuge in a rocky hut. The rain came pelting down, shattering the white Saint John roses clustered like sheaves of stars clinging to tree, rock, bush, and *pitaya* over the entire mountainside.

Below in the depths of the canyon, through the gauze of the rain they could see the tall, sheer palms shaking in the wind, opening out like fans before the tempest. Everywhere mountains, heaving hills, and beyond more hills, locked amid mountains, more mountains encircled in the wall of the sierra whose loftiest peaks vanished in the sapphire of the sky.

"Demetrio, please. For God's sake, don't go away! My heart tells me something will happen to you this time."

Again she was wracked with sobs. The child, frightened, cried and screamed. To calm him, she controlled her own great grief.

Gradually the rain stopped, a swallow, with silver breast and wings describing luminous charming curves, fluttered obliquely across the silver threads of the rain, gleaming suddenly in the afternoon sunshine.

"Why do you keep on fighting, Demetrio?"

Demetrio frowned deeply. Picking up a stone absentmindedly, he threw it to the bottom of the canyon. Then he stared pensively into the abyss, watching the arch of its flight.

"Look at that stone; how it keeps on going. . . ."

Chapter 7

It was a heavenly morning. It had rained all night, the sky awakened covered with white clouds. Young wild colts trotted on the summit of the sierra, with tense manes and waving hair, proud as the peaks lifting their heads to the clouds.

The soldiers stepped among the huge rocks, buoyed up by the happiness of the morning. None for a moment dreamed of the treacherous bullet that might be awaiting him ahead; the unforeseen provides man with his greatest joy. The soldiers sang, laughed, and chattered away. The spirit of nomadic tribes stirred their souls. What matters it whither you go and whence you come? All that matters is to walk, to walk endlessly, without ever stopping; to possess the valley, the heights of the sierra, far as the eye can read.

Trees, brush, and cactus shone fresh after rain. Heavy drops of limpid water fell from rocks, ocher in hue as rusty armor.

Demetrio Macías' men grew silent for a moment. They believed they heard the familiar rumor of firing in the distance. A few minutes elapsed but the sound was not repeated.

"In this same sierra," Demetrio said, "with but twenty men I killed five hundred Federals. Remember, Anastasio?"

As Demetrio began to tell that famous exploit, the men realized the danger they were facing. What if the enemy, instead of being two days away, was hiding somewhere among the underbrush on the terrible hill through whose gorge they now advanced? None dared show the slightest fear. Not one of Demetrio Macías' men dared say, "I shall not move another inch!"

So, when firing began in the distance where the

vanguard was marching, no one felt surprised. The recruits turned back hurriedly, retreating in shameful flight, searching for a way out of the canyon.

A curse broke from Demetrio's parched lips. "Fire at 'em. Shoot any man who runs away!"

"Storm the hill!" he thundered like a wild beast.

But the enemy, lying in ambush by the thousand, opened up its machine-gun fire. Demetrio's men fell like wheat under the sickle.

Tears of rage and pain rise to Demetrio's eyes as Anastasio slowly slides from his horse without a sound, and lies outstretched, motionless. Venancio falls close beside him, his chest riddled with bullets. Meco hurtles over the precipice, bounding from rock to rock.

Suddenly, Demetrio finds himself alone. Bullets whiz past his ears like hail. He dismounts and crawls over the rocks, until he finds a parapet: he lays down a stone to protect his head and, lying flat on the ground, begins to shoot.

The enemy scatter in all directions, pursuing the few fugitives hiding in the brush. Demetrio aims; he does not waste a single shot.

His famous marksmanship fills him with joy. Where he settles his glance, he settles a bullet. He loads his gun once more . . . takes aim. . . .

The smoke of the guns hangs thick in the air. Locusts chant their mysterious, imperturbable song. Doves coo lyrically in the crannies of the rocks. The cows graze placidly.

The sierra is clad in gala colors. Over its inaccessible peaks the opalescent fog settles like a snowy veil on the forehead of a bride.

At the foot of a hollow, sumptuous and huge as the portico of an old cathedral, Demetrio Macías, his eyes leveled in an eternal glance, continues to point the barrel of his gun.

RELATED READINGS

Continued

Zapata and the Mexican Revolution

Author John Steinbeck was fascinated with the Mexican revolutionary hero Emiliano Zapata, who, by the way, does not appear in The Underdogs. *After researching Zapata and Mexican history, Steinbeck documented his findings and wrote the screenplay for* Viva Zapata!

Zapata

by John Steinbeck

I

Mexican history is thought by most Americans to be a series of banditries and of small revolutions and revolts led by venal and self-interested men. The outbreaks and explosions are considered as comic opera movements of an inferior people. While it is true that there have been Mexican leaders who turned dishonest and who have sold their own people, even these leaders have been the products of a mass desire and a mass movement of the Mexican people. Because there is such a misconception of the forces in back of Mexican outbursts, it might be well to put in this introduction a short résumé of what has actually happened in Mexico.

When the Spanish conquerors under Cortez came to Mexico [in 1519], they found tribes and communities more or less like the Greek city-states, each one highly integrated, and each one possessing to a certain extent its own culture. Some of these states were tied together in larger leagues. There was nothing like the nation as we understand it today.

The Aztec group, a small and conquering people, had brought a great number of these cities and leagues and small groups under its sway, but the Aztec group was not a nation, in the sense that it had no intention of making the conquered peoples a part of itself. Indeed, the conquered peoples were simply tributary groups which paid the Aztecs to keep out of war, and failure to pay brought immediate reprisals—slaughter and slavery and the sacrifice to the gods of the best and most perfect individuals of the revolting people. But, since the domination of the Aztecs was harsh, and since its sole purpose was that of tribute, some of its subject states were in continual revolt against it.

It was only because of this hatred by the subject peoples of the Aztecs that Cortez was able to take Mexico. Had he been alone, and had he not had the help of Indian allies, he would never have been able to conquer the Mexican lands so easily; but every dominated people came to him because he spearheaded the revolt against the hated Aztec empire.

Cortez had three great weapons. He had firearms, he had smallpox, and he had the church, and of the three, the latter two were his greatest weapons, for the early authorities of the Spanish church, far from being cruel and rapacious, actually brought to Mexico a new sense of the dignity of men and brought, also, a concept of the importance of the individual soul—a thing which was completely foreign to Indian thinking. Indeed, the early members of the Spanish church allied themselves quite often with the Indians against the Spanish conquerors.

The cruelties and the slaveries of the Spanish domination were condemned equally by the Spanish throne and by the Spanish church. The villain here, as everywhere, and in all times, was greed.

A large part of the land was cut up into great holdings which were delivered over to those men who had fought in the conquest. Large numbers of career men came over from Spain to take what they could get out of the newly conquered country, and although slavery was not countenanced, something which was actual slavery was introduced—the Indians came with the land, and they were used with the land. They were worked in the mines and in the fields.

It is usual now, for ill-informed people, to say that the indigenous social and economic system of the original Indians of Mexico, and, indeed, of all America, was communistic. This is an oversimplification. Communal it was in a pre-Marxian sense, but communistic it was not. The system it most closely resembled was the early Greek city-state, or city group.

Land was not owned by individual men, in the sense that it could not be inherited by a man's son, but it surely was owned in the sense that he maintained it during his lifetime. Government was by village elders and by town elders. Groups of the older men held permanent positions in governing the communities. Land was allotted by the elders. In the long run, the land was actually owned by the community and was let out during the lifetime of a man to an individual for as long as he should make it produce. This was true of the producing lands. There were, in addition, the common lands, such as were in existence in England—grazing lands, woodlands, and so forth, but these came under other categories and were common to the use of all.

The laws were very definite and were largely traditional, like British Common Law. They were strictly enforced by the village elders. The laws were strangely general throughout the whole country and jumped even racial and tribal boundaries. They governed nearly all phases of human conduct. Thus, there was a law in the Aztec league, strictly enforced, that any man under fifty who got drunk was automatically executed, whereas after fifty he could get as drunk as he wanted to. The reason for this, of course, was that in a warlike nation the younger men must be ready for war and must be in good physical condition. After their time of military value was over, the state had little interest in what they did with their bodies.

The laws covered the most minute things, such as who owned an animal wounded by one arrow and who owned an animal wounded by two arrows when the animal was finally tracked down.

It is necessary to put in these details so that it can be realized how deeply ingrained in the Mexican people are their traditional laws, for many of those unwritten laws are still in force.

The Spanish conquerors, while they did break up the land to a large extent, had a healthy respect for the village lands, and it must be admitted that the church was one of the strong factors in maintaining the system of landholding, the economic and social systems they found there. The church had absolutely no patience with the indigenous religious system, but it went along very freely with the other forms it found there. The fact that certain religious practices, beliefs, and customs of the original people crept into the church could not be helped, because these things were so deeply ingrained in the people that they managed to maintain themselves against other customs. However, this has been the invariable practice of the church all over the world. What it cannot destroy, it must incorporate. For instance, it is true that certain hill peoples come still to the chapel of the Virgin of Guadalupe on December 12, and they not only dance before the altar but make symbols in colored sands on the church floor just as they did to another goddess who had had a temple in that same place before the Spaniards ever came; but now it is in the name of Christianity instead of in the name of the goddess Atlitl.

It must be remembered that the primary drive of the Spanish throne was one of conversion of the world to Christianity, its kind of Christianity and its form, and only secondarily was it interested in profits. The fact that this changed later does not in any way lessen the original and initial drive. It was a profoundly religious time. The monarchy and the Spanish church truly believed that their first mission was to convert the world. That this project required money and soldiers and arms and ships is self-evident, and this money had to come from some place since Spain was a very poor nation.

When the Spaniards had fastened themselves upon Mexico [during the first half of the 16th century], a gradual change took place. There was an immediate and quite general mixing of bloods. If the Spaniards had been content to accept the product of these bloods, they might still be holding Mexico, but the contrary was true. The Indian was not even a citizen. He was a native animal. The product of a marriage between a Spaniard and an Indian, while he had a slightly better social position, still held no office and was given no political preference of any kind. Officers were sent out from Spain. The Spanish colonies were the thriving ground for native Spaniards, practically never for either the intermixtures of Indian and Spanish, or even of the pure Spanish born in Mexico. Only a man born in Spain, of good blood, had any chance in the government of Mexico.

This was not true in the case of education. Very early, Indians entered the priesthood, and many of the first records, not only of the conquest but of the time that followed it, are the work of those first Indian Christian priests. It may be that they could not aspire to the highest ranks of the church nobility, but certainly they were used all over the country.

As far as the economy of Mexico went, it was a conquered and occupied country, and all of its products were considered to be the property of Spain and of people of Spanish blood, with the exception of the village lands, which were left and were protected.

Over the hundreds of years of the occupation of Mexico—and it was a true occupation—the great group of the mixed bloods increased, but their increase in numbers did not give them more preferment than they had had, political or social. They did not become the great middle class. They became the scholars, priests, the small storekeepers, but the threshold of advancement was very, very low. After a great number of years, they had become, in numbers at least and probably in intelligence, the dominant group in Mexico.

Then came two events which had a profound effect on this large group of Mexicans of mixed blood and native-born men of pure Spanish blood. The first of these great events was the American Revolution [1775–1783], and the second was the French Revolution [1789–1799].

A change had come over both the monarchy and the church, and in Spain at this time the two were more or less one. They had ceased to be missionary powers and had become economic systems whose purpose was the gathering of taxes, or tithes, and the accumulation of money and lands. These powers ignored the pressure of the growing group of intelligent Mestizos of Mexico. This group, stimulated by the two revolutions which had given them hope, broke into revolt, and, oddly enough, the leader of the revolt [1810] against the Spanish monarchy was a priest named Father

Hidalgo. It was an extremely popular revolt. Parts of the local church broke off from the parent church, and only in the hierarchy, in the highest groups, did the church side with the Spanish monarchy. In addition, the revolution of Mexico against Spain was backed by the great mass of the indigenous Indians, a faceless, nameless people who had never been recognized even as humans by any group except the church, and by them only more or less as humans who would assume their rightful stature in heaven after their death.

In addition, there was great sympathy for the Mexican Revolution against Spain from those two nations which had given them their initial hope, the new United States and the French Republic.

This was a revolution geographic in scope, but once it was accomplished another and perpetual revolt took its place, and this was not geographical. It was the revolt of the dispossessed against the group which held the resources of Mexico, and that revolt has continued during all Mexican history and still continues.

The revolutionary intent of the Mexican people, now as then, has not changed. It is a desire for the distribution of the land and resources of Mexico among the Mexican people. This hunger for land was the cause of the revolt of Morelos [1813], another priest incidentally, for the revolt of Benito Juárez [1867] against the reign of Maximilian, against Porfirio Díaz by Madero [1910–1911], and it continues into the present time.

Mexico, during all of its history, has had to contend against foreign domination, first Spain, then France, and then, in 1910, against a combination of Germany, France, the United States, and England. In every single case the revolts of the Mexican people have been aimed at land and, through land, at food.

In many cases the leaders of revolt have gone over to the other side and have become the dominant class against which a new revolt must be formed.

In this connection an interesting story was told me by Lincoln Steffens. He was a reporter at the time [1913] that Carranza was in a state of revolt, and he was on the train with Carranza after the final battles which put Carranza in power. The general said to him, "I know the pressures that will be put on me. How can I remain honest?" To which Mr. Steffens replied, "Why don't you leave the rifles with your men?"

"Why that?" Carranza asked.

"So they can kill you if you become dishonest," Steffens said.

Carranza nodded and said, "Yes, that might be a good way," but he didn't do it.

We come now to the time and the condition out of which our story grows, the story of Emiliano Zapata.

II

Benito Juárez was a pure Indian from the state of Oaxaca. His great admiration was for the American Constitution, and he attempted to build for Mexico a constitution like it. He was a friend of Abraham Lincoln and admired Lincoln above all other men. As a matter of fact, it was during Juárez administrations [1861–1864, 1867–1872] that Mexico grew conscious of constitutional law. But, as always, where it has been started, constitutional law runs afoul of those forces which, through possessions or positions, consider themselves outside the law.

The development of the Mexican constitution has been no different than that of any other. Although Juárez was able to get a constitution written, he was not able to get it enforced, and, after ensuing difficulties, another man—again an Indian—took over [in 1876], and his name was Porfirio Díaz. He soon became known as the Strong Man of Mexico.

He realized that Mexico was weak internally, and that she was surrounded by very strong and rich neighbors; and so he worked out a system for not only placating those rich neighbors but for buying them off, and trading with them. In the process he ignored his own country almost completely.

He established a system which is still called "Porfirismo," and his system was very simple. He collected a group of strong and intelligent men about him. He paid Mexico's debts to foreign nations; he distributed concessions of all kinds to foreigners, always for a price, but he delivered.

It is natural that the governments of Japan, Germany, France, England, and the United States admired him very much, for he had pacified the country. *How* he did it is another story, but people could go at will about Mexico without danger of being injured or robbed.

The interest on Mexico's debts to foreign nations was paid on time, and it was of little interest to those foreign governments how he got the money.

Foreign capital admired him very much, for it was able to invest its money in Mexico with some feeling that the properties bought would not be taken away. There was no interest in how Díaz got the property and the concessions to sell.

He was considered a great, strong, gifted man. He was given every decoration known, and nobody thought to investigate what his own people were going through, nor what was happening to them.

His methods were quiet and effective. If anyone disagreed with him in any matter, he first tried to buy that man, and if he did not succeed, the man disappeared and was not heard of again. It was clean and neat, and there was little publicity in any of it. There is on record a telegram he sent to one of his field officers which gave a long list of names, and his final sentence was "Catch and kill instantly."

He established a rural police, highly paid, made up mostly of criminals. These horsemen dispensed his justice and kept order, and their method of keeping order was by summary execution of anyone who interfered with their ways. They patrolled the roads, they acted as the private police for the large land-holders, they carried out the secret orders of President Díaz, and they executed his opponents, usually far in the desert—and only the buzzards had any record of what had happened.

Meanwhile, for a price, Porfirio Díaz distributed to foreign capital the oil, the minerals, and the land.

Mexico had abolished slavery twenty years before the American nation did, but soon a new slavery took its place, which was just as effective but was not called slavery. This was the slavery of debt. A man who owed money could not leave the land until it was repaid, and by a process of charging more for food and clothing than a man could possibly make, the probability that he could ever escape debt was very remote.

The rural police backed up these debts, so that if a man who owed a company store, or hacienda store, tried to leave that part of the country, to leave his work or his land and go somewhere else, he was instantly brought back and kept where he belonged, near the store. If he tried to escape too many times, the buzzards circled in the desert and that was that.

The pay and wages were exactly pegged to the point where a man could not possibly *ever,* in his whole life, get out of debt. It was not called slavery, but it was a most effective kind of slavery.

There was peace in Mexico. It was the peace of the rifle and the machete, but still there was peace, and it was said that you could ride along a lonesome road and never be robbed, and this was probably true.

By the use of his methods Porfirio Díaz stayed

in office for eight administrations [1876–1880, 1884–1911]. There was no question of re-election or election; he was simply declared president after a kind of token vote which meant nothing. But since all the foreign powers agreed that he was the best and strongest and wisest man, and since the vote was not widely distributed in Mexico, there was little doubt as to who was always going to be the next president.

His own people grew poorer and poorer, and fewer and fewer owned any land, and more and more of the Mexican land was distributed, for a price, to the large landholders. There were fewer little privately owned fields. Food supplies and minerals got into fewer hands, and those hands raised the prices, and wages never raised, and the food standard of Mexicans went down and down. What little educational standard there was disappeared completely, except among the very rich and among foreigners.

All of this was bad enough for the average Mexican, but Porfirio Díaz went even further. He began distributing the traditional village lands to the great landholders, and this was a crime so deep in the eyes of the village people that it cannot even be conceived. This was a violation of something that had been true for two thousand years. Not only were the village lands taken away, but in many cases the villages themselves were torn down and scattered to make room for more land for the landholders.

The tough and active rural police enforced these distributions and kept order, and there was peace, although many people had to die because of that peace.

Now, since this script [Steinbeck's screenplay] is to be written in microcosm, and since nearly all of its action takes place in a very small area, we shall move down to the state of Morelos, south of Mexico City, just over the range from the Valley of Mexico. It is a state which lies on a slope, and its temperatures go from cool-temperate into the tropics in a very short distance. It is a rich state, rich agriculturally and rich in silver. There is no oil there.

It is inhabited by a gentle, soft-spoken people of a tribe slightly different from the Aztec tribe. The men are great horsemen and great workers. They are filled with energy, but there's a gentleness about them that is unusual. Their faces are delicate, both those of the men and the women.

Their land—or rather the land of the state of Morelos—is well watered and rich, but in the time of Porfirio Díaz they did not own the land anymore. It had been discovered that sugar cane could be raised on these lands and that refined sugar brought a price which made it an easy competitor to silver mining and even to oil for profits. With such riches to be taken out of the raising and refining of sugar, the large landholders were not content that the village lands should remain in the hands of the Indians. And so, through the work of Porfirio Díaz, the haciendas, the great landholdings, spread out from their boundaries. In many cases the villages were burned and sugar cane was planted where the houses had stood, and the people who were evicted from their village lands had to go to work for the large landholders or run away and become fugitives.

The people of the state of Morelos are gentle and patient people, but their lives gradually became impossible under the system which was put in place by Porfirio Díaz and enforced by his troops and by his rural police.

Even the grazing land was in many cases taken away from the villages, so that the cows, upon which the Indians depended for their livelihood, had no place to feed. The slightest sign of rebellion or revolt was put down with a ferocity that was incredible. The Indians were treated like animals, they were driven like animals.

The events of this time are documented and quite provable. It is not propaganda in any sense.

In every town of even small size in Mexico there is a bandstand in the middle of the central plaza, and on several nights a week, usually on Thursday and on Sunday, a band plays in this stand. In the time of Porfirio Díaz the upper classes paraded around the bandstand, but the Indians were not permitted, except on the *outside* of the plaza; and if anyone, even while drunk, blundered in, he was bodily thrown out by the police who were constantly in attendance.

Any disagreement between the Indians and the owners of the land was instantly solved by the rural police, who were also the police of the landholders, and the Indians were never, never right. There were only three punishments for a recalcitrant man: he was put in the army, he was put in the rural police, or he was killed.

The haciendas became larger and larger. They actually were like medieval baronies. They had great houses, their sugar mills were usually on the property, they had slaves (or the slaves of debt), they had power for holding their slaves, and they actually had the power of life and death over the working people. No one ever questioned them.

I myself have seen records of this time on one of the great haciendas, or what is left of it. I remember a man's name on the record and his value. Against his name was put "zero." He was not worth anything, whereas the others were rated in what they were worth to the hacienda.

As this reign of Porfirio Díaz grew longer and longer and the people became hungrier and hungrier, and their sense of outrage greater, more and more pressure from the rural police had to be applied, and the punishments had to be more drastic and the killings more often.

Meanwhile, the outrage and the pressure and the simmering grew greater. This does not seem to have been realized by the men in power at that time. They felt that they had made a system which could survive indefinitely as long as they could get money from Germany and Japan and the United States. They completely ignored the explosive qualities in their own people; and why shouldn't they have so ignored them, for the people were disarmed, they had no weapons, they had no organization, they had no learning. The middle class was destroyed, the schoolteachers were dominated. The priests, those who favored the people, had little power—and there were many priests who favored the people. But the pressure of unrest grew and had to be kept down with more and more harsh methods all the time.

These were the conditions which brought about Emiliano Zapata and which brought about our story.

from Viva Zapata!

by John Steinbeck

Zapata emerged as the champion of landless peasants. In 1910 he joined the revolt that overthrew the dictatorship of Porfirio Díaz. Disenchanted with Francisco Madero, Mexico's newly elected president, Zapata and his followers (called zapatistas) refused to stop fighting until justice was restored. This meant using violence, if necessary, to force Madero to redistribute their lands.

CHARACTERS

Francisco Madero	president of Mexico (1911–1913) who ousted the dictator Díaz
Victoriano Huerta	Madero's general who became president of Mexico in 1913
Emiliano Zapata	a peasant leader of the Mexican Revolution
Eufemio Zapata	Emiliano Zapata's brother
Fernando Aguirre	a follower of Emiliano Zapata
Pablo Gomez	Emiliano Zapata's long-time friend

(*Dissolve to:*
Full Shot—Interior, a Government Office in Mexico City)

(*It is in a state of confusion.* Men *are moving filing cabinets. There is the characteristic constant repair that is invariable in Mexico; this always involves hammering. On one side a Work-*man *is measuring a pane for replacement, and we see that there is a bullet hole in the glass. We discover* Francisco Madero *pointing to a large map on the floor, around which stand* Emiliano *and* Fernando.)

Madero. Díaz was rottener than we knew. When Huerta pushed from the north, with Pancho Villa's help . . . and you, General, from the south, why, Díaz crumbled.

Emiliano (*very humbly*). If you will forgive me, sir, when will the village lands be given back? The country people are asking.

Madero. Now we must build—slowly and carefully!

Emiliano. Thank you. . . . But the country people want to know—

Madero. They will get their land, but under the law. This is a delicate matter. It must be studied.

Emiliano. What is there to study?

Madero. The lands must be given back under the law so that there will be no injustice. And speaking of lands, let me show you this. (*He turns to his desk, rifles through a number of maps, pulls out one and lays it on top.*) You see here, where these two streams meet? The land is very rich here, rich and level and well watered . . . and I'm told it has a good house on it. . . . Do you know what this is, General?

Emiliano. No, sir. . . .

Madero. This is your ranch and no one deserves it more than you.

Emiliano. My ranch?

Madero. Yes. It is a fine old custom to reward victorious generals . . .

(*Suddenly with a tremendous violence* Emiliano *bangs his gun on the floor. . . .*)

Emiliano. I did not fight for a ranch!

Madero (*quickly*). I don't think you know what I meant.

Emiliano (*topping him*). I know what you meant. . . .

(*Now he tries hard to get control of himself. Then he speaks . . . with difficulty.*)

Emiliano. Pardon me, sir. . . . But the land I fought for was not for myself!

Madero. But General—

Emiliano. What are you going to do about the land I did fight for?

Madero. General . . . General . . . that will be taken care of, believe me, in good time.

Emiliano. *Now* is a good time!

Madero. General Zapata, sit down.

Emiliano. I'm not tired.

Madero. This is a constitutional government, there is only one way to do these—(*There is a tremendous hammering.*) I can't think! I can't think here! This confusion! Get out . . . get out! (*He goes to the* Man *fixing a window and drags him to the door, herds the* Others *out . . . stops a Man with a paper. . . .*)

Madero. Give me these. I'll sign these now. Don't let anybody else in. . . .

(*Another Part of the Room*—Eufemio *and* Pablo Emiliano, *followed by* Fernando, *walks toward them.*)

Emiliano. This mouse in the black suit talks too much like Díaz.

Pablo. No, he's right. This is peace. We must work by law now.

Fernando. Law? Laws don't govern. Men do. And the same men who governed before are here now, in that room. They have his ear—it's obvious. They must be cleaned out. . . .

Emiliano. First, I want the land given back . . .

Fernando. And if Madero doesn't do it—

Emiliano. Yes?

Fernando. Then he is an enemy, too.

Pablo. But you're his emissary, his officer, his friend. . . .

Fernando. I'm a friend to no one—and to nothing except logic. . . . This is the time for killing!

Emiliano. Peace is very difficult.

(*During the foregoing* Eufemio *has turned aside, is standing by the map on the desk.* Emiliano *steps over to him.*)

Emiliano (*to* Eufemio). What do you think?

Eufemio (*sotto voce*). That's a nice piece of land he offered you. . . . What's the harm? You've never taken anything. And what have you got? Nothing!

(*Wider Angle*
The room has grown quiet. . . . Madero *comes toward them.*)

Madero. Now it's quiet. (*sinks wearily in his chair*) General Zapata—do you trust me?

(*Close Shot*—Emiliano, *silent.*)

(Fernando *and* Pablo *looking at* Emiliano.)

(Eufemio, *staring at his brother.*)

(*Group Shot—around* Madero.)

Madero. You must trust me! I promise you that my first preoccupation is with the land, but in a way that is permanent. But, before we can do anything by law, we must have law. We cannot have an armed and angry nation. . . . It is time, General, to stack our arms . . . in fact, that is the first step. . . . That is my first request of you. . . . Stack your arms and disband your army.

Emiliano. And who'll enforce the laws when we have them?

Madero. The regular army. The police!

Emiliano. But they're the ones we just fought and beat!

(*Now* Emiliano *picks up his rifle, advances slowly toward* Madero.)

Emiliano. Give me your watch!

Madero. What?

Emiliano. Give me your watch.

(*This is an order. Fiercely given and meant.* Madero *slowly removes his watch from his breast pocket and holds it out.* Emiliano *takes it, looks at it*).

Emiliano. It's a beautiful watch . . . expensive. . . . (*now quickly*) Now, take my rifle.

(*He reverses his gun and offers it.* Madero *does not take it.*)

(Zapata *lays the gun on the desk, with the barrel pointing toward his own chest.*)

Emiliano. Now . . . you can take your watch back. . . . but without that—(*He points to the gun.*) Could you?

Madero (*chuckling*). You draw a strong moral . . .

Emiliano. You ask us to disarm . . . are you sure we could get our land back, or keep it, if we disarm?

Madero. It's not that simple, there's the matter of time.

Emiliano. Time . . . yes, time . . . time is one thing for a lawmaker, but to a farmer there is a time to plant and a time to harvest. . . . You cannot plant in harvest time.

Madero. General Zapata, do you trust me?

Emiliano. Just the way my people trust me. I trust you and they trust me as long as we keep our promises. (*reaches for his gun*) Not a moment longer.

(*He thinks a moment, turns, and starts toward the door. Fernando, Pablo, and Eufemio follow.*)

Madero. Where are you going?

Emiliano. I'm going home.

Madero. What will you do there?

Emiliano. I'll wait. But not for long!

(*The door closes on The Four.*)

(*Another Door to the Room*
It opens and there enters a Man we have not seen before. He is Victoriano Huerta, one of Madero's generals from the north. A hard, cruel, ambitious man. An aide now steps in behind him. Huerta starts forward.)

(*Angle at Madero's Desk, as Huerta enters, followed by several tough, hardened Generals. As the scene progresses, they gradually step in near to Madero, so that they seem to be surrounding him.*)

Huerta. Kill that Zapata now. Save time, lives, perhaps your own.

Madero. Were you listening, General Huerta?

Huerta. I advise you to shoot Zapata now.

Madero. I don't shoot my own people.

Huerta. You'll learn . . . or you won't learn. . . .

Madero. He's a fine man.

Huerta. What does that mean?

Madero. I mean he's an honest man.

Huerta. What has that got to do with it??!! A man can be honest and completely wrong!

Madero. I trust him.

Huerta. To do what? I feel it is essential that I take my troops down to Morelos and help him decide to disarm.

(*There is a knock on the door, then the door opens. It is* Pablo. *He sees who's there.*)

Pablo. Oh. . . .

Madero. Come in. . . .

(*Angle at Door*
Pablo *looks at* Huerta *uncertainly. . . . He hesitates, still by the door.* Madero *crosses over to him warmly. . . .*)

Pablo (*to* Madero). I thought—

Huerta: You can speak freely.

Madero. I want to speak to General Zapata again. . . . Ask him to come back, will you?

Pablo. He won't come back. He's stubborn, you know

. . . but if you could come down to Morelos, he's different there. You know, his whole life has been fighting. (*sotto voce*) He can hardly read. (*urgently*) He needs you. He may not know it yet, but he needs you to help him. And he can learn. . . he wants to. . . and, if you'll excuse me, you need him too.

(Madero *thinks for a moment; then looks at* Pablo.)

Madero. I will come. . . .

Pablo. Thank you. (*bows, then formally*) With your permission, sir . . . (*to* Huerta) Excuse the interruption, please.

(*This means:* "May I leave now?" Madero *answers by stepping over to* Pablo *and embracing him.*)

Madero. Tell him I will come. . . .

(Pablo *exits.* . . . Madero *turns back to* Huerta.)

Madero (*to* Huerta). I will do it without troops. . . . Troops are not necessary . . . these are fine men. . . .

(Madero *turns to exit, pauses.*)

Madero. You know, General Huerta, there is such a thing as an honest man. . . .

(Madero *smiles and exits.*)

(*Close Shot*—Huerta *and* Aide
Huerta *whoops.*)

Huerta. What a fool! Oh, the odor of goodness! Give me a drink. . . .

(*The* Aide *gets out a bottle.* . . .)

Huerta. We'll never get any place as long as Zapata is alive. He believes in what he's fighting for. . . .

Aide. So does Madero, General. . . .

Huerta. Oh, I know, but he's a mouse . . . he can be handled. . . . Zapata's a tiger . . . you have to kill a tiger!

(*Camera moves downward, and we see that* Huerta *is standing on the map, his feet firmly planted on the State of Morelos.*)

(*Dissolve to:*
Exterior, the Plaza of a Town)

(*In front of a table where there are* Clerks, *slowly passes a line of* Zapatista Fighters *surrendering their guns. As the weapons are surrendered, the name of each owner is written in a book and on a tag tied to the gun. The line stretches all the way across the plaza.*)

(*Medium Shot—Group at Table*
As each man surrenders his weapon it is thrown into a farm cart. Behind the table stand Emiliano, Madero, Pablo, *and* Eufemio. (*The* Soldadera *is in the background.*)

Madero. You see, they feel all right about giving up their arms now that I have explained it to them.

Pablo. He explained it very well, didn't he, Emiliano?

(Emiliano *is silent.* Madero *watches him.*)

Madero. They've accepted it. Have you?

Emiliano. I've been fighting so long. I don't understand peace.

Madero. Peace is the hard problem. Many men have been honest in war. . . . I often wonder how a man can stay honest under the pressure of peace. . . .

(*A* Man *in the line who is just about to give up his rifle holds it up. . . .*)

Man. Let us keep these.

Madero (*turns*). What do you mean?

Eufemio. He means, so he can shoot you if you turn crooked!

(*He suddenly bursts into crude laughter and goes off. The* Man *hands over his rifle and moves along.* Madero *looks at* Emiliano *and they laugh, too. . . .*)

Emiliano (*he points to a grizzled* Old Man *who is next in line*). He doesn't look like much, but he's one of the best fighters we had. Aren't you, Apolonio?

Apolonio. No.

(*He gives up his rifle and moves on. They all laugh.*)

Emiliano (*to* Madero). Did I tell you about the little boy who got my horse?

Madero. Yes, you did. Where is he? I'd like to meet him.

Emiliano (*throwing it away*). He's dead. (*thinks a second, then:*) We were never able to find the horse.

(*Another Angle*
Emiliano *indicates a* Woman *who is bringing three rifles. Nods at her with his head.*)

Madero. That woman has three rifles!

Emiliano. Lost a husband and two sons—killed.

(*The* Woman *deposits the guns.* Madero's *eyes fill with tears. He moves toward the* Woman, *reaching in his pockets for something to give her. All he can find is his watch. He hands it to her. She puts her hand under her apron.*)

Madero. Take it!

Woman. Oh, no, it is too valuable.

(Madero *takes her hand and puts the watch in the palm and closes the fingers over it and says, harshly:*)

Madero. As valuable as your sons?

(*Camera moves into close shot of* Emiliano *and* Pablo. *We see that* Emiliano *likes and believes in* Madero. Pablo *sees this and is glad.*)

(*Wider Angle*
Fernando, *followed by* Eufemio, *comes into the scene, and gestures to* Emiliano.)

Fernando (*anxiously*). Emiliano, come here!

Emiliano. What do you want?

Fernando (*changes his mind. Speaks sullenly, gesturing toward* Madero). Ask him!

Emiliano. Use respect!

Madero (*with a gesture of helplessness*). What is it . . .?

Eufemio. General Huerta's forces are coming through the pass!

Fernando (*to* Madero). Pretend you don't know it!

Madero. Oh, no, they're not—no, they can't!

Emiliano (*to* Fernando). How do you know?

(Fernando *points to three dusty and perspiring* Scouts *who are drinking water thirstily.*)

Eufemio. The Scouts! Three regiments with artillery.

Emiliano. Who posted Scouts?

Fernando. I did.

Emiliano. You?

Fernando (*indicating* Madero). I don't trust him. And I'm right! Look at him!

(Madero *is bewildered. The* Others *stare at him. A* Citizen, *unaware of what is happening, approaches* Madero.)

Citizen (*to* Madero). I want to shake the hand of our Liberator. I can tell my children.

(*Automatically,* Madero *extends his hand.*)

Madero (*as though to himself*). Troops are coming, Huerta has disobeyed orders. . . .

Citizen. What—what do you say, sir?

Madero. Thank you very much. (*the Citizen goes*) I'll have to go and stop them. Huerta wouldn't dare.

(*He rises, walks away a few steps, hesitates—confused and bewildered.*)

Fernando (*to* Emiliano). Don't let him get away!

Pablo. You must trust Madero, Emiliano! He can bring us peace.

Fernando (*interrupting*). Peace! . . . Three regiments coming down on us! Peace! You ugly little ape, you fool!

(Pablo *goes for his knife and for* Fernando's *neck. . . . A knife has suddenly appeared in the hands of the* Soldadera.)

Emiliano. Pablo! Stop it! Put that knife away! Fernando, send cavalry to engage—see to the outposts. . . .

Fernando. Yes, General. . . . (*starts away, stops—to* Madero) Go on back to Mexico City. . . . Huerta is a strong man. . . he'll gobble you up. . . .

(Emiliano *interrupts violently.*)

Emiliano. Fernando!
(Fernando *exits. . . .*)

Emiliano. Pablo! The snipers. Flank the road. . . .

Eufemio (*sotto voce, indicating* Madero). Might be a good idea to finish him off! What do you say?

(*Before* Emiliano *can reply,* Madero *comes back to him.*)

Madero. Emiliano, believe in me! I will stop the troops.

Emiliano. I hope so. . . . But if you can't, I will! (*to* Eufemio) Come on.

(*They exit.*)

(*Another Angle*
Emiliano *is issuing orders. The line reverses. Guns are issued. An electric quality comes into the square like a storm breaking.* Horses *and* Riders *move about with great speed.*)

(*Medium Shot*—Madero *and* Pablo (*the* Soldadera *in the background*). Madero *nervously wipes his forehead.* Pablo *looks at him sympathetically.*)

Madero. General Huerta must have misunderstood.

Pablo. I'll talk to Emiliano. I'll bring you two together again. . . .
(*He hurries off, followed by the* Soldadera. Madero *still stands there, confused and bewildered.*)

(*Dissolve to:*
Long Shot—*Mounted* Federal Scout, *coming down a road which leads to a river.*)

(*Medium Shot*—*the* Scout *as he stops at the edge of the river, looks carefully in all directions; then he turns in his saddle, signals in the direction of a heavily wooded area.*)

(*Long Shot*—*Shooting toward the Wooded Area*
A mounted Federal Column *emerges from the woods, comes toward the river.*)

(*Full Shot of the Column Crossing the River.*
As they are in the middle of the stream, suddenly they are fired upon. There is a wild thrashing about of the frightened Horses. *The* Federales *look around, trying to find out where the firing is coming from.*)

(*Another Angle around the River.*
From the tall grass the figures of the Zapatistas *rise, continue firing. At the height of this battle, we cut to:*)

(*Close Shot—*Emiliano
on horseback, his field glasses held to his eyes, watching the battle. He lowers the glasses, and a look of satisfaction comes over his face. The way he planned it, that way it worked!)

(*Dissolve to:*
A Small Room in the National Palace—Mexico City
It is sparsely but adequately furnished. Two Soldiers *stand at the door guarding it. At a bare table sits* Madero, *staring straight ahead. He's in a highly nervous state . . . almost hysteria.*
There's a knock at the door. The Two Soldiers *open it a slit, and then, seeing who it is, open it wide. An immaculately dressed* Senior Officer *enters.* Madero *almost runs to him.*)

Madero. Did you see him? Did you see Huerta?

Officer. Yes, my President. . . .

Madero. How does he explain this? Why am I a prisoner here?

Officer (*suavely*). You're no longer a prisoner, my President.

Madero. But they won't let me leave! I've been in this room for days!

Officer. Of course. He's guarding you for your safety. You have enemies outside.

Madero. What enemies?

Officer. Zapata, Pancho Villa, they've all turned against you. But don't worry. General Huerta loves you. He will protect you. You must agree—here you have been safe.

Madero. Why doesn't he give me safe conduct to the Port? When is he going to let me see him?

Officer. Tonight. He asked me to take you to him.

(*Frantically* Madero *runs to a mirror. We watch him close up as he ties his cravat, straightens his worn hair. . . .*)

(*Dissolve to:*
A Military Car with a Driver
In the back seat, Huerta *and an* Aide, *smoking cigars.* Huerta *looks at a watch.*)

Huerta. They are late.
(*A* Soldier *runs up to the car.*)

Soldier. They're coming. . . .
(Huerta *throws away his cigar. Looks out the window of the car.*)

(*An Open Car Drives into View, Its Lights Dimmed*
In the back seat between Two Officers *sits* MADERO. *His face is full of anticipation. The car stops;* Madero *looks around questioningly at an* Officer.)

Officer. Get out.

Madero. Is he here?

Officer: Get out.
(Madero *raises his head and sees the wall of the penitentiary, before which the scene is being played.*

Suddenly the whole plot and all knowledge of it crash in on his mind.)

(*Close-up*—Madero.
He knows he's doomed.)

(*Wider Angle*
Suddenly the Two Officers *give him a boost.* Madero *seems to accept his fate. Almost aloofly he steps from the car.* Two Soldiers *appear from the darkness, take him by the arms and conduct him almost gently in front of the car. They leave him. Suddenly the full headlights turn on him. They blind him. He looks around, for where to go. . . . Takes a few tentative steps . . . turns back toward the car and starts to speak. . . .*)

Madero. My friend, what—
(*The extra loud horn of the car sounds, drowning out his voice.* Madero *turns away hopelessly, his body waits for the bullets he knows are coming.*)

(Huerta's *Car*
Huerta *is listening tensely. . . . There is a volley of shots offscreen. The sound of the automobile horn dies out. The open car, in which* Madero *came, crosses behind.*)

Huerta (*to his* Aide). So much for the mouse. Now we'll go for the Tiger.
(*He takes a fresh cigar, bites off the end of it.*)

(*Dissolve to:*
Zapata's *Headquarters—the Courtyard of a Ruined Hacienda A court-martial is taking place.* Zapata, *looking much older and much more worn, is sitting at a table. Behind him stands* Fernando, *who looks fiercer and meaner. All around in a great circle stand the* Men *of his army listening. They are really battle-worn. A high wind is blowing.* Eufemio *is conducting the court-martial.*

Medium Shot—at Table
Zapata *looks at a* Guarded Man, *who stands in front of the table.*)

Clerk of the Court. Consorting with the enemy. He was seen talking to an officer of Huerta's army.

Eufemio (*leaning toward* Prisoner). We were ambushed. We know that now! What have you got to say for yourself?

Prisoner (*with a certain amount of arrogance*). Why shouldn't I talk to him? He was my brother-in-law. He brought me a message from my wife.

Eufemio. How did he know where to find you?

Prisoner (*pause—he is trapped*). I sent word.

Eufemio (*rising*). You sent word and we were ambushed!

Prisoner (*again defensive*). I haven't seen my wife in two years!

Eufemio (*to* Guards). Shoot him!

Emiliano. Wait a minute.
(*An electric pause, as they all look toward him. The* Prisoner's *face lights up with hope.*)

Emiliano (*to Prisoner*). Look behind you.

(*Long Shot*
What he sees: A long line of white-clad Zapatistas, *each carrying the body of a* Dead Zapatista *up a hill* (*moving away from the camera*) *and disappearing over the brow of the hill. Another Line* comes back, moving toward us.)

(*Back to Scene*)

Zapata. Two hundred and forty-four fighting men. We planned a surprise. Huerta was ready for us. (*he speaks to* All the Men) When they killed Madero, we had to start all over again. We lost many men. It was necessary. But *this* was useless. Two hundred and forty-four good farmers, your relatives, with victory in their mouths, will never chew it. (*to the* Prisoner, *with sudden violence*) Now do you see why we have hard discipline? You told your wife where we would be—and—(*he turns to* Eufemio) Shoot him.

(*The* Prisoner *is led away.* Emiliano *looks up and sees a group of* Federal Soldiers *under guard.*)

Captain of the Guard. Thirty-two deserters, my General. They want to come over to us. . . .

Emiliano (*he has said this many times recently, there have been many* Deserters *brought to him*). If you want to fight for your land and your liberty, you're welcome. You'll be watched. There's no mercy for traitors. None! It's easier to come over to us now that we are winning, isn't it? (*to* Fernando) Take care of them.

(Fernando *gestures to another* Man, *who comes forward and escorts the* Deserters *away.*)

Emiliano (*to* Eufemio). Go on.

Eufemio (*to* Clerk). Next!

(*A* Prisoner *is brought forward.*)

Clerk. This one broke our law against looting.

Emiliano (*rising, to* Eufemio). I'll sleep a little.

(He takes from Eufemio a bottle of strong liquor (which Eufemio has been liberally using). He goes off, Fernando follows him.)

(*Moving Shot*—Emiliano *and* Fernando
Fernando *watches him.*)

Fernando. Putting it off?

(*They go up to a door opening in the thick wall and enter. Camera stops on the* Soldadera, *who is squatting against the wall on the side of the door. Her face, as ever, is expressionless. By now she is really worn. Much time and misery have passed. In her rebozo, slung over one shoulder, lies an* Infant. *She pays no attention to it. . . . She is making tortillas. She doesn't look up as the men go by.*)

(*Small Dark Room*
Pablo *is sitting on a bench with a* guard *on either side of him. He looks up as* Emiliano *and* Fernando *enter.* Emiliano *takes a seat, avoids* Pablo's *glance.*)

Pablo. You look tired, Emiliano.
(Emiliano *doesn't answer.* Fernando *takes charge.*)

Fernando. He met with the enemy: I have witnesses!
(*In the scene that follows,* Fernando *addresses* Pablo, *but* Pablo *never talks to* Fernando *nor looks at him. He speaks to* Emiliano.)

Pablo. You don't need witnesses, Emiliano. Just ask me. It's true I met Madero before he was killed.

Fernando. You met him many times!

Pablo. Many times, Emiliano.

Fernando. Even after Madero had signed orders to destroy us!

Pablo. That was at the end, Emiliano. Madero wasn't himself. He was trying to hold Huerta in check. Then Huerta killed him. He was a good man, Emiliano. He wanted to build houses and plant fields. And he was right. If we could begin to build—even while the burning goes on. If we could plant while we destroy . . .

Fernando. This is your defense?
(*Sound of execution offstage.*)

Pablo. You and Villa will beat Huerta, soon! But then,

there will be other Huertas, always other Huertas! Killing only makes new enemies, Emiliano. . . .

Fernando. You deserted our cause!

Pablo. Our cause was land—not a thought, but corn-planted earth to feed the families. And Liberty—not a word, but a man sitting safely in front of his house in the evening. And Peace—not a dream, but a time of rest and kindness. The question beats in my head, Emiliano. Can a good thing come from a bad act? Can peace come from so much killing? Can kindness finally come from so much violence? [He looks now directly into Emiliano's immobile eyes.] And can a man whose thoughts are born in anger and hatred, can such a man lead to peace? And govern in peace? I don't know, Emiliano. You must have thought of it. Do you know? Do you know?
(*Silence.* Emiliano *does not answer. A pause . . . offscreen—a fusillade is heard. The execution squad.* Fernando *looks at* Emiliano.)

Fernando (*slowly*). Two hundred and forty-four of our fighting men were killed this morning. We planned to surprise the enemy. They surprised us!
(*Pause.*)

(*Close Shot*—Emiliano *and* Pablo)

Pablo (*sensing what is happening behind* Emiliano's *mask*). Emiliano, we've been friends since we guarded the corn against the blackbirds.

Emiliano (*slowly*). You knew our rule against consorting with the enemy?

Pablo. Yes, my General.

Emiliano. And yet you ignored it?

Pablo. Yes, my General.

Fernando's voice. Shall I call the squad?

Pablo (*with pleading in his eyes*). Emiliano, not strangers. Do it yourself. Do it yourself!

(Fernando *gets up, silently, and goes outside.*)

(*Full Shot—Room*
Fernando *gestures to the* two guards, *who leave. Fernando follows.* Emiliano *and* Pablo *are alone.*)

(*Exterior, Small Dark Room*
Fernando *comes out, closes the door.*)

(*Close-up—*Soldadera
She *looks up at him for a moment.*)

(*Back to Scene*
Fernando *stands just outside the door to the small dark room. A* Courier, *guarded, comes up.*)

Courier (*to Fernando*). Where's General Zapata? I have a message of great importance from General Villa.

Fernando. General Zapata is busy.

(*From inside comes the sound of a shot. The* Soldadera *dumps the charcoal from her brazier; she stands up and, gathering her food, walks away.*)

Fernando (*to courier*). General Zapata will see you now.

The Festival of Bullets

by Martin Luis Guzmán
Translated by Seymour Menton

The Underdogs *captures the violence and
brutality of the Mexican Revolution as
Demetrio and his band of rebels clash with
enemy soldiers. The following nonfiction
account also depicts the savage and cruel
character of the Mexican Revolution as
Rodolfo Fierro orchestrates a "festival of
bullets."*

My interest in Villa and his movement often made
me ask myself, while I was in Ciudad Juárez, which
exploits would best paint the Division of the North:
those supposed to be strictly historical or those rated
as legendary; those related exactly as they had been
seen, or those in which a touch of poetic fancy brought
out their essence more clearly. The latter always
seemed to me truer, more worthy of being considered
history.

For instance, where could one find a better painting
of Rodolfo Fierro—and Fierro and Villa's movements
mirrored each other down to the last detail—than in
the account of how he carried out the terrible orders
of his chief after one of the battles, revealing an
imagination as cruel as it was creative in death de-
vices. This vision of him left in my soul the sensation
of a reality so overwhelming that the memory of it
lives forever.

That battle, which was successful in every way, had
left no less than five hundred prisoners in Villa's

hands. Villa ordered them divided into two groups: the Orozco volunteers, whom we called "Reds," in one, and the Federals in the other. And as Villa felt himself strong enough for grandiose acts, he decided to make an example of the first group and to act more generously toward the second. The "Reds" were to be executed before dark; the Federals were to be given their choice of joining the revolutionary troops or returning home, after promising not to take up arms against the Constitutionalist cause.

Fierro, as might have been expected, was put in charge of the execution, and he displayed in it that efficiency which was already winning him great favor with Villa, his "chief," as he called him.

The sun was beginning to set. The revolutionary forces, after breaking camp, were slowly gathering in the little village that had been the objective of their offensive. The cold, penetrating wind of the Chihuahuan plains began to blow and the groups of cavalry and infantry huddled next to the walls of the houses. But Fierro—whom nothing and nobody ever held back—was not going to flee from a cool breeze that at most meant frost that night. He rode along slowly on his short-rumped horse, with the edge of his sarape against the horse's dark hair dirtied from the dust of the battle. The wind was hitting him smack in the face, but he neither buried his chin in his breast nor raised the folds of his sarape around his face. He carried his head high, his chest thrown out, his feet firm in the stirrups, and his legs gracefully flexed under the campaign equipment that hung from the saddle straps. The barren plain and an occasional soldier that passed at a distance were his only spectators. But he, perhaps unconsciously, reined his horse to make him show his gaits as though he were on parade. Fierro was happy; the satisfaction of victory filled his being; and to him victory was complete only when it meant the utter rout of the enemy; and in this frame of mind even the buffeting of the wind, and continuing to ride fifteen consecutive hours in the saddle, produced physical sensations that were exhilarating. The rays of the pale setting sun, a sun prematurely enveloped in incendiary flames, seemed to caress him as they fell.

He reached the corral where the three hundred "Red" condemned prisoners were shut up like a herd of cattle, and he stopped a moment to look at them over the fence rails. In outward appearances those three hundred Huerta supporters could have passed for revolutionaries. They were of the fine Chihuahua breed, tall, lean bodies with strong necks and well-formed shoulders on vigorous supple backs. As Fierro looked over the small captive army and sized up its military value and bravery, a strange pulsation ran through him, a twitching that went from his heart or from his forehead out to the index finger of his right hand. Involuntarily the palm of his hand reached out for the butt of his pistol.

"Here's a battle for you," he thought.

The cavalrymen, bored with their task of guarding the prisoners, paid no attention to him. The only thing that mattered to them was the annoyance of mounting this tiresome guard, all the worse after the excitement of the battle. They had to have their rifles ready on their knees, and when an occasional prisoner left the group, they aimed at him with a determined air, and, if necessary, fired. A wave would then ripple through the vague perimeter of the mass of prisoners, that retracted to avoid the shot. The bullet would either go wide of its mark or bring one of them down.

Fierro rode up to the gate of the corral. He shouted to a soldier, who let down the bars, and went in. Without removing his sarape from his shoulders, he leaped off the horse. His legs were numb with cold and weariness; he stretched them. He arranged his two pistols. Next he began to look slowly over the pens, observing their layout and how they were divided up. He took several steps over to one of the fences without letting go of the reins. He slipped something out of one of the saddle bags into the pockets of his jacket and crossed the corral at a short distance from the prisoners.

Actually, there were three corrals that opened into one another, with gates and a narrow passageway between. From the one where the prisoners were kept, Fierro went into the middle enclosure, slipping through the bars of the gate. He went straight over to the next one. There he stopped. His tall, handsome figure gave off a strange radiance, something superior, awe-inspiring, and yet not out of keeping with the desolation of the corral. His sarape had slipped down until it barely hung from his shoulders; the tassels of the corners dragged on the ground. His gray, broad-brimmed hat turned pink where the slanting rays of the setting sun fell on it. Through the fences the prisoners could see him at a distance, his back turned toward them. His legs formed a herculean compass that glistened: it was the gleam of his leather chaps in the late afternoon light.

About a hundred yards away, outside the corrals, was the officer of the troop in charge of the prisoners. Fierro saw him and signaled him to come closer, and the officer rode over to the point of the fence closest to Fierro. The latter walked toward him. The two began to talk. In the course of the conversation, Fierro pointed out different spots in the enclosure in which he was standing and in the one next to it. Then he described with hand gestures a series of operations, which the officer repeated, as though to understand them better. Fierro insisted two or three times on what seemed to be a very important maneuver, and the officer, now sure about his orders, galloped off toward the prisoners.

The Festival of Bullets   195

Fierro then turned back toward the center of the corral, studying once more the layout of the fence, and other details. That corral was the largest of the three, and the first in line, nearest to the town. On two sides gates opened into the fields; the bars of these, though more worn—from greater use—than those of the farther pens, were of stronger wood. On the other side, there was a gate that opened into the adjoining corral, and on the far side the fence was not of boards, but was an adobe wall, no less than nine feet high. The wall was about sixty yards long, twenty of which formed the back of a shed or stable, with a roof that sloped down from the top of the wall and rested on the one side on the taller end posts of one of the fences that bordered on the open fields and on the other, on a wall, also of adobe, which came out perpendicular from the wall and extended some fifteen yards toward the middle of the corral. Thus, between the shed and the fence of the adjoining corral, there was a space enclosed on two sides by solid walls. In that corner the afternoon wind was piling up rubbish and clanging an iron bucket against the well curb with an irregular rhythm. From the well curb rose two rough forked posts, crossed by a third, from which a pulley and chain hung, which also rattled in the wind. On the very top of one of the forks sat a large still whitish bird, hardly distinguishable from the twisted points of the dry pole.

Fierro was standing about fifty steps from the well. He rested his eyes for a moment on the motionless bird, and as though its presence fitted in perfectly with his thoughts, without a change of attitude or expression, he slowly pulled out his pistol. The long, polished barrel of the gun turned into a pink finger in the fading sunlight. Slowly it rose until it pointed in the direction of the bird. The shot rang out—dull and diminutive in the immensity of the afternoon—and the bird dropped to the ground. Fierro returned his pistol to its holster.

At that moment a soldier jumped over the fence into the yard. It was Fierro's orderly. He had jumped from such a height that it took him several seconds to get to his feet. When he finally did, he walked over to where his master was standing.

Without turning his head Fierro asked him:

"What about them? If they don't come soon, we aren't going to have time."

"I think they're coming."

"Then you hurry up and get over there. Let's see, what pistol have you got?"

"The one you gave me, Chief. The Smith and Wesson."

"Hand it over here and take these boxes of ammunition. How many bullets have you got?"

"About fifteen dozen today, Chief, that I've been able to scrounge up. Some of the other men found lots of them, but I didn't."

"Fifteen dozen? I told you the other day that if you kept on selling ammunition to buy booze, I'd put a bullet through you."

"No, Chief."

"What do you mean: 'No, Chief'?"

"I do get drunk, Chief, but I don't sell the ammunition."

"Well, you watch out, 'cause you know me. And now you move lively so this stunt will come out right. I fire and you load the pistols. And mind what I tell you: if on your account a single one of the Reds gets away, I'll put you to sleep with them."

"Oh, what a chief!"

"You heard what I said."

The orderly spread his blanket on the ground and emptied out the boxes of cartridges that Fierro had just given him. Then he began to take out one by one the bullets in his cartridge belt. He was in such a hurry that it took him longer than it should have. He was so nervous that his fingers seemed all thumbs.

"What a chief!" he kept thinking to himself.

In the meantime, behind the fence of the adjoining corral the soldiers who were guarding the prisoners began to appear. They were on horseback, with their shoulders showing above the top fence rail. There were many others stationed along the two other fences.

Fierro and his orderly were the only ones inside the corral: Fierro with a pistol in his hand, and his sarape fallen at his feet; his orderly squatting and lining up the bullets in rows on his blanket.

The leader of the troop rode up through the gate that opened into the next corral and said:

"I've got the first ten ready. Shall I turn them loose for you?"

"Yes," answered Fierro, "but first explain things to them. As soon as they come through the gate, I'll begin to shoot. Those that reach the wall and get over it are free. If any of them don't want to come through, you shoot them."

The officer went back the same way he came, and Fierro, pistol in hand, stood attentive, his eyes riveted on the narrow space through which the prisoners were going to break out. He stood close enough to the dividing fence so that, as he fired, the bullets would not hit the Reds who were still on the other side. He wanted to keep his promise faithfully. But he was not so close to the fence that the prisoners could not see, the minute they came through the gate, the pistol that was leveled at them twenty paces away. Behind Fierro the setting sun turned the sky a fiery red. The wind kept blowing.

In the corral where the prisoners were herded, the sound of words grew louder, words that the whistling of the wind destroyed, like those used by herders rounding up cattle. It was a hard task to make the three hundred condemned men pass from the last to the middle corral. At the thought of the torture awaiting them, the whole group writhed with the convulsions of a person in the grip of hysteria. The soldiers of the guard were shouting and every minute the rifle shots seemed to gather up the screams as with a whiplash.

Out of the first prisoners that reached the middle corral a group of soldiers separated ten. There were at least twenty-five soldiers. They spurred their horses on to the prisoners to make them move; they pushed the muzzles of their carbines against their bodies.

"Traitors! Dirty bastards! Let's see how you can run and jump. Get a move on, you traitor!"

And in this way they made them advance to the gate where Fierro and his orderly were waiting. Here the resistance of the Reds grew more intense; but the horses' hoofs and the carbine barrels persuaded them to choose the other danger, the danger of Fierro, who was not an inch away, but twenty paces.

As soon as they appeared within his range of vision, Fierro greeted them with a strange phrase, a phrase both cruel and affectionate, containing both irony and hope:

"Come on, boys; I'm the only one shooting, and I'm a bad shot."

The prisoners jumped like goats. The first one tried to throw himself on Fierro, but he had not taken three leaps before he fell, riddled by bullets from the soldiers stationed along the fence. The others ran as fast as they could toward the wall—a mad race that must have seemed to them like a dream. On seeing the well curb, one tried to find refuge there: he was the first one hit by Fierro's bullet. The others fell as they ran, one by one; in less than ten seconds Fierro had fired eight times, and the last of the group dropped just as his fingers were touching the adobe bricks that by a strange whim separated at that moment the zone of life from the zone of death. Some of the bodies still showed signs of life; the soldiers finished them off from their horses.

And then came another group of ten, and then another, and another, and another. Fierro's three pistols—his own two and that of his orderly—alternated with precise rhythm in the homicidal hand. Six shots from each one, six shots fired without stopping to aim and without pause, and then the gun dropped on to the orderly's blanket, where he removed the exploded caps, and reloaded it. Then, without changing his position, he held out the pistol to Fierro, who took it as he let the other fall. Through the orderly's fingers passed the bullets that seconds later would leave the prisoners stretched lifeless, but he did not raise his eyes to see the men fall. His whole being seemed to concentrate on the pistol in his hand, and on the bullets, with their silver and burnished reflections, spread out on the ground before him. Just two sensations ran through his bones: the cold weight of the bullets that he was putting into the openings of the cylinder, and the contact with the smooth warm surface. Over his head one after another rang out the shots of his "chief," delightfully engrossed in his target practice.

The panic-stricken flight of the prisoners toward the wall of salvation—a fugue of death within a terrifying symphony in which the two themes of the passion to kill and the infinite desire to live struggled with each other—lasted almost two hours.

Not for one moment did Fierro lose his precise aim or his poise. He was firing at moving human targets, targets that jumped and slipped in pools of blood and amidst corpses stretched out in unbelievable postures, but he fired without any emotion except that of hitting or missing. He even calculated the deflection of the bullets caused by the wind, and corrected it with each shot.

Some of the prisoners, crazed by terror, fell to their knees as they came through the gate: the bullets made them keel over. Others danced about grotesquely behind the shelter of the well curb until the bullet cured them of their frenzy or they dropped wounded into the well. But nearly all rushed toward the adobe wall and tried to scale it by climbing over the warm, damp, steaming heaps of piled-up bodies. Some managed to dig their nails into the dirt on the top of the wall, but their hands, so actively clutching for life, soon fell lifeless.

A moment arrived in which the mass execution became a noisy tumult, punctuated by the dull snap of the pistol shots, muted by the immense voice of the wind. On one side of the fence could be heard the shouts of those who were trying to flee from death only to die; on the other, those who resisted the pressure of the horsemen and tried to break through the wall that pushed them on toward that terrible gate. And to the shouts of one group and the other were added the voices of the soldiers stationed along the fences. The noise of the shooting, Fierro's marksmanship, and the cries and frantic gestures of the dying men had worked them up to a pitch of great excitement. They greeted with joyful exclamations the somersaults of the falling bodies; they shouted, gesticulated, and laughed uproariously as they fired into the heaps of human flesh in which they noted the slightest evidence of life.

In the last squad of victims there were twelve instead of ten. The twelve piled out of the death pen, falling over one another, each trying to shield himself with the others, as he raced ahead in the horrible race. In order to go forward they had to hop over the piled-up corpses, but that didn't prevent the bullets from hitting the mark. With sinister precision they hit them one by one and left them halfway to the wall, arms and legs outstretched, embracing the mass of their motionless companions. But one of them, the only one left alive, managed to reach the very top of the wall and to clear it. The firing stopped suddenly and the gang of soldiers crowded into the corner of the adjoining corral to see the fugitive.

It was beginning to get dark. It took the soldiers a little while to focus their vision in the twilight. At first they could see nothing. Finally, far off, in the vastness of the semidark plain they managed to make out a moving spot. As it ran, the body bent so far over that it almost seemed to crawl along on the ground.

A soldier took aim. "It's hard to see," he said as he fired.

The shot died away in the evening wind. The moving spot fled on.

Fierro had not moved from his place. With his arm exhausted, he let it hang limp against his side for a long time. Then he became aware of the pain in his forefinger and raised his hand to his face; he could see in the sunlight that his finger had become somewhat swollen. He rubbed it gently between the fingers and the palm of his other hand. And there he stood for quite a while engrossed in the gentle, soft massage. Finally he stooped over and picked up his sarape, which he had taken off at the beginning of the executions. He threw it over his shoulders and started walking to the shelter of the stable. But after a few steps he turned to his orderly:

"As soon as you're finished, bring up the horses."

And he continued on his way.

The orderly was gathering up the exploded caps. In the next corral the soldiers had dismounted and were talking or singing softly. The orderly listened to them silently and without raising his head. Then he rose slowly to his feet. He gathered up the blanket by its four corners and threw it over his shoulder. The empty caps clattered within like a dull rattle or jingle.

It was dark. A few stars glimmered, and on the other side of the fence the tips of the cigarettes were also glimmering. The orderly started to walk heavily and slowly and, half feeling his way, went to the last of the corrals and then returned leading the horses by the bridle—his master's and his own; across one of his shoulders swung the haversack.

He made his way over to the stable. Fierro was sitting on a rock, smoking in the dark. The wind whistled through the cracks in the boards.

"Unsaddle the horse and make up my bed," ordered Fierro. "I'm so tired I can't stand up."

"Here in this corral, chief? Here. . . ?"

"Yes, here. Why not?"

The orderly did as he was ordered. He unsaddled the horse and spread the blankets on the straw, making a kind of pillow out of the haversack and the saddle. Fierro stretched out and in a few minutes was asleep.

The orderly lighted his lantern and bedded the horses for the night. Then he blew out the light, wrapped himself in his blanket, and lay down at his master's feet. But a moment later he got up again, knelt down, and crossed himself. Then he stretched out on the straw again.

Six or seven hours went by. The wind had died down. The silence of the night was bathed in moonlight. Occasionally a horse sneezed nearby. The radiance of the moon gleamed on the dented surface of the bucket that hung by the well and made clear shadows of all the objects in the yard except the mounds of corpses. They rose up, enormous in the stillness of the night, like fantastic hills, with strange and confused outlines.

The silvery blue of the night descended on the corpses like the clearest light. But imperceptibly that light gradually turned into a voice, a voice equally unreal as the night. The voice grew distinct; it was a voice that was barely audible, faint, painful, and dying, but tenuously clear like the shadows cast by the moon. From the center of one of the mounds of corpses the voice seemed to whisper:

"Ow! Ow! . . ."

Then it was silent and the silvery blue of the night became only light again. But the voice was heard a second time:

"Ow! . . . Ow! . . ."

The heaped-up bodies, stiff and cold for hours, lay motionless in the corral. The rays of moonlight penetrated them as though they were an inert mass. But the voice sounded again:

"Ow. . . . Ow. . . . Ow. . . ."

And this last groan reached the spot where Fierro's orderly lay sleeping and brought him out of sleep to the consciousness of hearing. The first thing that came to his mind was the memory of the execution of the three hundred prisoners; the mere thought of it kept him motionless on the straw, his eyes half open and his whole body and soul fixed on the lamenting voice:

"Ow. . .please. . . ."

Fierro tossed on his bed.

"Please. . .water. . . ."

Fierro awoke and listened attentively.

"Please. . .water. . . ."

Fierro stretched out his foot and nudged his orderly.

"Hey, you. Don't you hear? One of those dead men is asking for water."

"Yes, chief."

"You get up and put a bullet through the sniveling son of a bitch. Let's see if he'll let me get some sleep then."

"A bullet through who, chief?"

"The one that's asking for water, you idiot. Don't you understand?"

"Water, please," the voice repeated.

The orderly took his pistol from under the saddle and, clutching it, got up and left the stable in search of the corpses. He was shivering with fear and cold. He felt sick to his soul.

He looked around in the moonlight. Every body he touched was stiff. He hesitated without knowing what to do. Finally he fired in the direction from which the voice seemed to come. The voice was heard again. The orderly fired a second time. The voice died away.

The moon sailed along on the endless space of its blue light. Under the roof of the stable Fierro slept.

The Dictators

by Pablo Neruda
Translated by Robert Bly

In The Underdogs *Cervantes tells Demetrio, "We are not fighting to dethrone a miserable murderer, we are fighting against tyranny itself." How do people suffer under the tyrannical rule of dictators?*

LOS DICTADORES

Ha quedado un olor entre los cañaverales:
una mezcla de sangre y cuerpo, un penetrante
pétalo nauseabundo.
Entre los cocoteros las tumbas están llenas
5   de huesos demolidos, de estertores callados.
El delicado sátrapa conversa
con copas, cuellos y cordones de oro.
El pequeño palacio brilla como un reloj
y las rápidas risas enguantadas
10   atraviesan a veces los pasillos
y se reúnen a las voces muertas
y a las bocas azules frescamente enterradas.
El llanto está escondido como una planta
cuya semilla cae sin cesar sobre el suelo
15   y hace crecer sin luz sus grandes hojas ciegas.
El odio se ha formado escama a escama,
golpe a golpe, en el agua terrible del pantano,
con un hocico lleno de légamo y silencio.

THE DICTATORS

An odor has remained among the sugarcane:
a mixture of blood and body, a penetrating
petal that brings nausea.
Between the coconut palms the graves are full
5   of ruined bones, of speechless death-rattles.
The delicate dictator is talking
with top hats, gold braid, and collars.
The tiny palace gleams like a watch
and the rapid laughs with gloves on
10   cross the corridors at times
and join the dead voices
and the blue mouths freshly buried.
The weeping cannot be seen, like a plant
whose seeds fall endlessly on the earth,
15   whose large blind leaves grow even without
      light.
Hatred has grown scale on scale,
blow on blow, in the ghastly water of the
      swamp,
with a snout full of ooze and silence.

When Evil-Doing Comes Like Falling Rain

by Bertolt Brecht
Translated by John Willett

In The Underdogs *Demetrio compares the revolution to "a volcano in eruption . . . a cataclysm," and so he and the other rebels "keep on killing and killing." Brecht, in this poem, sees a similar evil in Nazi Germany. How does one endure the cataclysm of killing, the genocide, in a revolution or a war?*

Like one who brings an important letter to
    the counter after office hours: the counter
    is already closed.
Like one who seeks to warn the city of an
    impending flood, but speaks another
    language. They do not understand him.
Like a beggar who knocks for the fifth time
    at a door where he has four times been
    given something: the fifth time he is
    hungry.
Like one whose blood flows from a wound
    and who awaits the doctor: his blood goes
    on flowing.
5 So do we come forward and report that evil
    has been done us.

The first time it was reported that our friends were being butchered there was a cry of horror. Then a hundred were butchered. But when a thousand were butchered and there was no end to the butchery, a blanket of silence spread. When evil-doing comes like falling rain, nobody calls out 'stop!'

When crimes begin to pile up they become invisible. When sufferings become unendurable the cries are no longer heard. The cries, too, fall like rain in summer.

"It's Terrible" or "It's Fine"

by Mao Zedong

Is revolutionary violence justified? Mao Zedong (1893–1976), leader of China's communist revolution, presents his views on this issue.

The peasants' revolt disturbed the gentry's sweet dreams. When the news from the countryside reached the cities, it caused immediate uproar among the gentry. Soon after my arrival in Changsha, I met all sorts of people and picked up a good deal of gossip. From the middle social strata upwards to the . . . right-wingers, there was not a single person who did not sum up the whole business in the phrase "It's terrible!" Under the impact of the views of the "It's terrible!" school then flooding the city, even quite revolutionary-minded people became downhearted as they pictured the events in the countryside in their mind's eye; and they were unable to deny the word "terrible." Even quite progressive people said, "Though terrible, it is inevitable in a revolution." In short, nobody could altogether deny the word "terrible."

But . . . the fact is that the great peasant masses have risen to fulfill their historic mission, and that the forces of rural democracy have risen to overthrow the forces of rural feudalism. . . . This is a marvelous feat never before achieved, not . . . in thousands of years. It's fine. It is not "terrible" at all. It is anything but "terrible." "It's terrible!" is obviously a theory for combating the rise of the peasants in the interests of the landlords; it is obviously a theory of the landlord class for preserving the old order of feudalism and obstructing the establishment of the new order of democracy, it is obviously a counterrevolutionary theory. No revolutionary comrade should echo this nonsense.

If your revolutionary viewpoint is firmly established and if you have been to the villages and looked around, you will undoubtedly feel thrilled as never before. Countless thousands of the enslaved—the peasants—are striking down the enemies who battened on their flesh. What the peasants are doing is absolutely right; what they are doing is fine! "It's fine!" is the theory of the peasants and of all other revolutionaries.

Every revolutionary comrade should know that the national revolution requires a great change in the countryside. The Revolution of 1911 [which overthrew the 2000-year-old imperial system and attempted to establish a republic] did not bring about this change; hence its failure. This change is now taking place, and it is an important factor for the completion of the revolution. Every revolutionary comrade must support it, or he will be taking the stand of counterrevolution.

The Question of "Going Too Far"

Then there is another section of people who say, "Yes, peasant associations are necessary, but they are going rather too far." This is the opinion of the middle-of-the-roaders. But what is the actual situation?

True, the peasants are in a sense "unruly" in the countryside. Supreme in authority, the peasant association allows the landlord no say and sweeps away his prestige. This amounts to striking the landlord down to the dust and keeping him there. The peasants threaten, "We will put you in the other register!" They fine the local tyrants and evil gentry, they demand contributions from them, and they smash their sedan-chairs. People swarm into the houses of local tyrants and evil gentry who are against the peasant association, slaughter their pigs, and consume their grain. They even loll for a minute or two on the ivory-inlaid beds belonging to the young ladies in these households. . . . At the slightest provocation, they make arrests, crown the arrested with tall paper hats, and parade them through the villages, saying, "You dirty landlords, now you know who we are!" Doing whatever they like and turning everything upside down, they have created a kind of terror in the countryside. This is what some people call "going too far," or "exceeding the proper limits in righting a wrong," or "really too much."

Such talk may seem plausible, but in fact it is wrong. First, the local tyrants, evil gentry, and lawless landlords have themselves driven the peasants to this. For ages they have used their power to tyrannize the peasants and trample them underfoot; that is why the peasants have reacted so strongly. The most violent revolts and the most serious disorders have invariably occurred in places where the local tyrants, evil gentry, and lawless landlords perpetrated the worst outrages.

The peasants are clear-sighted. Who is bad and who is not, who is the worst and who is not quite so vicious, who deserves severe punishment and who deserves to be let off lightly—the peasants keep clear accounts, and very seldom has the punishment exceeded the crime.

Second, a revolution is not a dinner party, or writing an essay, or painting a picture, or doing embroidery; it cannot be so refined, so leisurely and gentle, so temperate, kind, courteous, restrained, and magnanimous. A revolution is an insurrection, an act of violence by which one class overthrows another. A rural revolution is a revolution by which the peasantry overthrows the power of the feudal landlord class. Without using the greatest force, the peasants cannot possibly overthrow the deep-rooted authority of the landlords, which has lasted for thousands of years. The rural areas need a mighty revolutionary upsurge, for it alone can rouse the people in their millions to become a powerful force.

Tienanmen Square: A Soldier's Story

by Xiao Ye
Translated by Jay Sailey

In The Underdogs *Solís tells Cervantes about an irony of the revolution: "What a colossal failure we would make of it, friend, if we, who offer our enthusiasm to crush a wretched tyrant, became the builders of a monstrous edifice holding one hundred or two hundred thousand monsters of exactly the same sort." Is this what happened in China's Revolution?*

Xiao Ye was born in China, the son of an army general. When he was fourteen he joined the People's Liberation Army of China. He served in the army for five years.

Mr. Xiao was in Beijing at the time of the Tienanmen Square demonstrations and the subsequent crushing of the protest by the People's Liberation Army. He witnessed the profound impact these events had on the Chinese people. His time in the army made the clash between citizens and soldiers particularly painful.

"Xiao Ye" is a pseudonym. The author is an exile who currently lives in the United States.

His story follows:

"How could the People's Liberation Army attack us, the citizens of Beijing?"

"Never in the history of China have the Army's tanks been turned against the Chinese people!"

"Our leaders are like fathers, and the soldiers are like uncles to us—how could they betray us?"

These and many other expressions of shock echoed throughout Beijing the morning after the violent suppression of demonstrations for political freedom in Tienanmen Square on June 4, 1989. After fifty days of jubilant protest by students and workers, many of whom had set up squatters' housing in the square, the demonstration had become the focus of international attention and an embarrassment to the Chinese leaders. Whatever the degree of dissent in the square, however, whatever level of anger the Party leaders might have felt toward the demonstrators, no one believed it possible that the Army would open fire on their own.

Days after that very occurrence, I stood watching the troops marching across the now depopulated square. My mind turned back to the early days of the protest.

Even then I had an uneasy premonition of the violence to come. And when I first spoke with my father about the demonstration, that uneasiness grew. As a retired Army general who had devoted his entire life to the Party and the revolution, Father regarded anyone who questioned the Party as a counter-revolutionary. In his view, the students and workers in the square were intent on dismantling everything he and his comrades had striven to create for more than fifty years. He listened with tightlipped disapproval as I described what was happening at Tienanmen.

I knew his attitudes to be in keeping with those of his generation, a reflection of the resentment harbored toward the demonstrators by the gerontocracy in power. My father could not accept the idea that the protesters might be seeking a new vision for China. For him, the issue was black and white: The demonstrators did not respect those who had sacrificed everything for this same China, for the sake of *these very demonstrators* and their happiness. If they respected all that had been done on their behalf, he reasoned, those rebels would not now be embarrassing the Party. I felt my enthusiasm evaporate in the face of his obvious displeasure.

The days wore on and the demonstration flourished. Many became increasingly hopeful that political change and new political freedoms would come peacefully to China. I continued to visit my father, but we found less and less to say to each other.

One night the lights in the square were turned off. No one knew what to make of it. Tanks and armored personnel carriers rolled into the square. Soldiers began firing on the dissenting citizens of Beijing, some of whom were in their makeshift tents. The soldiers, some fresh from the provinces, many with a wild roving fear, fired into the unarmed crowd and people scattered, tripping in the darkness as they tried to escape. People were shaken and stunned. Their assumptions about the Army's role as protector of the people were shattered as surely as the demonstration was brutally overrun. China was a family at war with itself, and Tienanmen was the dragon biting its own tail. But that circular motion of frustration was the outcome of a process that had other beginnings.

Standing now looking at the square, I thought about the soldiers of Tienanmen. I recognized their uniforms, every button and seam; I knew the shape, weight, and capability of their automatic weapons; many times over I had heard the command that caused them to fire. I, too, had once been a soldier in the People's Liberation Army.

I still remember clearly the morning I said good-bye to my father and set off to join the Army. I was all of fourteen. Father had held a high position in the government but had been criticized during the Cultural Revolution and had been sent to the countryside to do manual labor. For a similar reason, Mother had been sent for re-education to a village more than forty miles away. Father and I were living alone in a small hut on a hill overgrown with weeds.

I walked into the hut, pack on my back, to say good-bye. My father was sitting there on the dilapidated bed with a gloomy look on his face. I felt for the first time that I stood before him as a man. I was going to join the Army, his Army, leaving home as he had done more than thirty years earlier.

It was a great day for me. For my generation, which came of age in the 1970s, to become a soldier in the Army and serve the Party was the noblest ideal. Catching a lift on a truck heading toward the train station, I was filled with the passionate certainty that I had taken the first step on the road to my destiny.

Five nights later I was hundreds of miles away, on Shanxi Road in Nanjing, in a fashionable neighborhood where high officials lived. I stood on the porch of one of my father's old wartime comrades, a general and chief of staff to the commander of the Nanjing military district. Fingering the letter of introduction that my father had written for me, I nervously rang the bell. The guard who answered the door told me that the general and his family were at the theater. I told him the reason for my visit, but he closed the door on me. I sat down beside the door and fell asleep.

I don't know how much time passed before I was jolted awake by a shout. The general and his family had returned home to find someone sitting in the shadows near the door. Thinking I might be an assassin, the general's bodyguard had immediately drawn his gun. Later that night the general apologized and explained that another high official, someone who had been on the wrong side of the political struggle between Chairman Mao and Marshal Lin Biao, had only recently been assassinated in his home.

The general took me with him to military district headquarters a few days later. We walked into the main building, which looked more like a mansion than an office, with its hardwood tables and chairs and comfortable sofas. Another officer arrived with two teenaged boys, also sons of the general's wartime companions. The general had arranged for all three of us to join the Army together.

The general had personally inducted the sons of so many high-level cadres and military officials that they could form an entire company. During the conscription season at the beginning of each year his home was filled with them. The general was a man who valued friendship. In those days there was no better way to prove his friendship than to assist people's children into the Army. Perhaps in the complex web of human relationships it was one of the most important routes to officialdom in China.

The unit I joined was directly attached to the Nanjing military district, and my camp was situated about twenty-five miles southeast of Nanjing. I was introduced to the staff officer, a heavyset man with a kind, avuncular attitude toward his men. He politely asked me what I wanted to do. I said anything at all would be fine: menial duties, cooking, raising pigs. If only I could be a soldier and fight the Russians and the Americans, I said, any amount of misery or fatigue wouldn't matter. He looked both surprised and pleased.

He asked me my age. I lied and said that I was sixteen. He thought for a moment and decided to send me to Company X. That was his old outfit, he told me, and I knew from this assignment that he liked me. He summoned a soldier, who escorted me to the company barracks. I was delighted. I was finally a soldier.

In China to say, "I was a soldier" is like saying, "I can take hardship." Not only is military life tense, but the training is primitive and spartan. Chinese soldiers have a saying, "If you sweat a lot in ordinary times, you bleed less in wartime." The principles of training serve to increase the pressure and hardships that the soldier is able to tolerate. This better equips him for war.

Military life was very strictly regulated. Our clothing, the length of our hair, the way we walked, the respect we showed to senior officers—all were specifically regulated. Everyone got up, trained, ate, and went to bed at the same time. If it was not time for lights out, you could not even touch the side of your bed.

Every morning at 5:00 a.m. we would be awakened by a bugle reveille. I would leap out of bed, throw on my shirt, button it up, pull on my trousers and button them up, and then fasten my belt as I rushed out of the room. If I were fast enough there would be time to pee in the big vat around which a line of men had already formed; otherwise I'd have to hold it in while we did our morning run of four to five miles. Needless to say, that was not easy.

Later I became more experienced. When I heard the wake-up signal I pulled on my shirt, trousers, and hat, hung my battle gear around my neck, and raced out of the barracks, buttoning and straightening my uniform as I ran. That way, I wouldn't be late.

Antitank training was an important part of our military training. In those days, when all we had at our disposal were firebombs, hand grenades, and bazookas, we also had a saying: "A squad should swap their equipment and lives to disable an enemy tank." We practiced different means of getting close enough to a tank—sometimes even running up to it—to be able to blow it up. Our drills included even more primitive practices such as throwing Molotov cocktails or inserting wooden poles in the tread of a tank to stop it.

It was felt that by using these tactics we could s ap the enemy's strength and stop his advance. Like everyone else, I resolved to sacrifice my life for this purpose. Diagrams of the Soviet T62 and the American M1 tanks were posted all over the camp, so all of the soldiers were acquainted with their capabilities and firepower.

In 1970, the year I entered the army, a special effort was made to upgrade the fighting capacity of the troops. The military units set up special training groups called "guidance teams." The members were selected from the technical core of each company, who were given intensive training so that they could return to their units and serve as trainers. I was chosen to be on a regimental guidance team.

Our squad instructor was as strong as an ox and swarthy, brainless but knowledgeable about military technology, an old pro. He had fought in the Civil War. His military record was good, but because he was not educated, he was never promoted. He didn't care a whit about the political discussions bandied about the camp, and it didn't seem to matter to him with whom he was fighting. As long as there was fighting and he had a part in it, he was satisfied.

He was very demanding of the men on his team. He would often point out a high hill and order us to use tactics to secure it within a given number of minutes. When we practiced shooting from a prone position, he made us crawl in the hot sun for several hours. If someone got tired and tried to sneak in a little shifting movement, he would give him a swift kick. When he ordered us to charge forward and dive to the ground, he wanted us to dive very fast and continue to slide headlong for a few yards, since that was the only way he could determine our speed. The skin on my knees and elbows would be scraped off, but as he said, the speed with which you can get down is critical on the battlefield, because losing a few seconds could cost your life. He taught us: "To be a good soldier you should stand like a pine tree and sit like a grandfather clock, awe-inspiring and stern." I learned quite a lot about fighting from him.

One of the things I liked least was being taken out of camp to live and train in the open. This type of training began in 1970, when Mao Zedong observed that during the Civil War he himself had never stayed in a military camp. He ordered the Army to train in the wilderness so that we would be tough in time of war.

Thus it happened that every winter all field armies held large-scale maneuvers. Each day we normally marched 20 to 25 miles, sometimes more. Every man had to carry his gun, four hand grenades, more than 100 bullets, a small iron shovel, several pounds of dry rice, and a canteen. In addition we carried a satchel containing a military comforter, a change of uniform, and a pair of rubber-soled shoes. A raincoat that doubled as a tarpaulin was tied to the top of our pack. Taken together, this equipment weighed between 85 and 100 pounds. We also had to take turns carrying the ammunition crates.

These marches involved crossing mountain roads and dirt roads. Sometimes there was no road at all. When crossing mountainous regions we had to use our arms and legs like gorillas, taking a step and then grabbing a tree, or crawling up a cliff.

Hiking at night was particularly dangerous, especially when it was raining in the mountains. All lights were forbidden in order to guard against aerial reconnaissance, so you could only follow the sound of the feet ahead of you and rely on your senses. Slipping and sliding in the mud, I would grit my teeth at every pace, never sure where I might put my foot down.

One night I heard a sloshing sound ahead of me. I reached out and grabbed at what I could, a foot that had slipped, and I slid after it. The file of men ahead of us had made a turn before a precipice, but the soldier in front of me had not seen it and had kept going straight. Three or four of us fell off the cliff with him into a wet rice paddy.

We usually developed bleeding blisters on our feet after a few days of this kind of hiking. Our feet were a mass of soggy peeling flesh and blood, and the pain was almost unbearable. Empty vehicles followed after us, and anyone who wanted to could get a lift, but very few chose to. We considered the physical challenge a means of tempering ourselves for the sake of the Party. That attitude was encouraged by the political cadres, who walked back and forth among the ranks exhorting us: "This is the point at which the Party is testing you." In that kind of situation, no one wanted to look bad.

After walking for ten hours, my pack and the gun on my shoulder seemed to weigh a thousand pounds. My feet felt as if they had been cast in lead. Every step took great effort. My greatest desire was to lie down and rest, even if it was raining or snowing, even if it meant that I would die. Several times I started to doze off; the man behind me would bump into me and wake me up.

Of course, when we had reached our goal we still could not rest. We had to build fortifications, make camouflage, set up a communications system, and in all respects prepare ourselves to fight a battle. It was exhausting.

Once when a platoon commander was trying to make a telephone call the female operator asked why he was so short of breath. He answered grumpily, "We've just marched more than 30 miles; who wouldn't be short of breath?" Later he was reprimanded because of that one sentence: A revolutionary soldier should not care how much he has endured; he must never complain.

We were also required to devote a lot of time to political studies. Our texts were Mao's writings as well as editorials from the official newspapers. Each company had lessons in basic political terms and information, which we were usually required to memorize. When I joined the army the influence of the Cultural Revolution was still strong, and every evening we lined up under Mao's portrait. The squad leader would speak for us, "reporting to Chairman Mao" what we had done for the sake of the revolution that day, what mistakes we had made, and what we resolved to do tomorrow.

The Army also had a policy of "recalling the suffering of the old society." The political officers often invited a toothless old woman and other peasants from a neighboring village to tell us about life before the revolution. The old woman would wipe away her tears as she spoke about the cruelty of the past and how the landlord had mistreated the peasants. This kind of indoctrination, repeated day after day, reinforced the belief that life under the Communist Party leadership was the best in the world and that it was our duty as soldiers to preserve the system.

All of these traditions were intended to foster in us a sense of honor at being revolutionary soldiers; to fan our hatred of class enemies; and to teach us restraint, self-sacrifice, and obedience to the Party and the needs of the revolution.

It had a powerful effect. For instance, in the 1970s China and the Soviet Union sent high-range artillery and guided missile units to Vietnam to support the Vietcong. During an American bombing raid it was discovered that the Chinese artillery had too short a range and could not reach the bombers. Destruction over the target area was intense. Despite the ineffectiveness of their weapons, the Chinese soldiers continued to fire upward at the American planes, shouting quotations from Mao: "Be firm in resolve, don't fear sacrifice, push aside all difficulties, fight for victory!" The Soviet guided missile units nearby stared at this with jaws dropping, doubtless thinking that their Chinese colleagues had lost their minds.

And during the days in Tienanmen, once again the soldiers did not complain. They obediently drove forward, aimed, and opened fire on command. In light of their training, how could it have been otherwise?

It is interesting, as I sit here in my study in the United States, to think of those soldiers in the square. Many of the protesters that the soldiers faced had themselves been soldiers and received Army training. I believe it was precisely that Army experience that allowed the demonstrators in and around Tienanmen to be so effective in disabling more than 1,000 of the military vehicles that appeared on the streets of Beijing.

When people in the West ask how I feel about the events in Tienanmen Square and the future of China, I am inevitably confronted with the contradiction between repulsion at the political blindness of the troops and the shedding of blood, and the deep affection I have for my time in the military and my life with my comrades. Rage at the soldiers who fought

against unarmed protesters is mixed with compre-
hension of their reflex to obey.

What of my old father, the general? To this day our
love is intact even though he still approves of the way
the events in the square were handled, making the
subject taboo between us. You ask me about China
and I will tell you it is as complex as the emotions of
a man sent to the fields to do hard labor for crimes he
didn't commit, all the while approving of the decision
to punish him since it was made by the Party. As
complex as a son who wanted nothing more than to
serve, but who found that service in challenging the
old to bring about the new.

How Much Land Does a Man Need?

by Leo Tolstoy
Translated by Louise and Aylmer Maude

For Mexican peasants, owning land was the key to regaining their power. In the following story, a Russian peasant's wish for land changes his life in surprising ways.

An elder sister came to visit her younger sister in the country. The elder was married to a tradesman in town, the younger to a peasant in the village. As the sisters sat over their tea talking, the elder began to boast of the advantages of town life: saying how comfortably they lived there, how well they dressed, what fine clothes her children wore, what good things they ate and drank, and how she went to the theatre, promenades, and entertainments.

The younger sister was piqued, and in turn disparaged the life of a tradesman, and stood up for that of a peasant.

"I would not change my way of life for yours," said she. "We may live roughly, but at least we are free from anxiety. You live in better style than we do, but though you often earn more than you need, you are very likely to lose all you have. You know the proverb, 'Loss and gain are brothers twain.' It often happens that people who are wealthy one day are begging their bread the next. Our way is safer. Though a peasant's life is not a fat one, it is a long one. We shall never grow rich, but we shall always have enough to eat."

The elder sister said sneeringly:

"Enough? Yes, if you like to share with the pigs and the calves! What do you know of elegance or manners! However much your goodman may slave, you will die as you are living—on a dung heap—and your children the same."

"Well, what of that?" replied the younger. "Of course our work is rough and coarse. But, on the other hand, it is sure, and we need not bow to anyone. But you, in your towns, are surrounded by temptations; to-day all may be right, but to-morrow the Evil One may tempt your husband with cards, wine, or women, and all will go to ruin. Don't such things happen often enough?"

Pahóm, the master of the house, was lying on the top of the stove and he listened to the women's chatter.

"It is perfectly true," thought he. "Busy as we are from childhood tilling mother earth, we peasants have no time to let any nonsense settle in our heads. Our only trouble is that we haven't land enough. If I had plenty of land, I shouldn't fear the Devil himself!"

The women finished their tea, chatted a while about dress, and then cleared away the tea-things and lay down to sleep.

But the Devil had been sitting behind the stove, and had heard all that was said. He was pleased that the peasant's wife had led her husband into boasting, and that he had said that if he had plenty of land he would not fear the Devil himself.

"All right," thought the Devil. "We will have a tussle. I'll give you land enough; and by means of that land I will get you into my power."

II

Close to the village there lived a lady, a small landowner who had an estate of about three hundred acres. She had always lived on good terms with the peasants until she engaged as her steward an old soldier, who took to burdening the people with fines. However careful Pahóm tried to be, it happened again and again that now a horse of his got among the lady's oats, now a cow strayed into her garden, now his calves found their way into her meadows—and he always had to pay a fine.

Pahóm paid up, but grumbled and, going home in a temper, was rough with his family. All through that summer, Pahóm had much trouble because of this steward, and he was even glad when winter came and the cattle had to be stabled. Though he grudged the fodder when they could no longer graze on the pasture-land, at least he was free from anxiety about them.

In the winter the news got about that the lady was going to sell her land and that the keeper of the inn on the high road was bargaining for it. When the peasants heard this they were very much alarmed.

"Well," thought they, "if the innkeeper gets the land, he will worry us with fines worse than the lady's steward. We all depend on that estate."

So the peasants went on behalf of their Commune, and asked the lady not to sell the land to the innkeeper, offering her a better price for it themselves. The lady agreed to let them have it. Then the peasants tried to arrange for the Commune to buy the whole estate, so that it might be held by them all in common. They met twice to discuss it, but could not settle the matter; the Evil One sowed discord among them and they could not agree. So they decided to buy the land individually, each according to his means; and the lady agreed to this plan as she had to the other.

Presently Pahóm heard that a neighbor of his was buying fifty acres, and that the lady had consented to accept one half in cash and to wait a year for the other half. Pahóm felt envious.

"Look at that," thought he, "the land is all being sold, and I shall get none of it." So he spoke to his wife.

"Other people are buying," said he, "and we must also buy twenty acres or so. Life is becoming impossible. That steward is simply crushing us with his fines."

So they put their heads together and considered how they could manage to buy it. They had one hundred rúbles laid by. They sold a colt and one half of their bees, hired out one of their sons as a laborer and took his wages in advance; borrowed the rest from a brother-in-law, and so scraped together half the purchase money.

Having done this, Pahóm chose out a farm of forty acres, some of it wooded, and went to the lady to bargain for it. They came to an agreement, and he shook hands with her upon it and paid her a deposit in advance. Then they went to town and signed the deeds; he paying half the price down, and undertaking to pay the remainder within two years.

So now Pahóm had land of his own. He borrowed seed, and sowed it on the land he had bought. The harvest was a good one, and within a year he had managed to pay off his debts both to the lady and to his brother-in-law. So he became a landowner, ploughing and sowing his own land, making hay on his own land, cutting his own trees, and feeding his cattle on his own pasture. When he went out to plough his fields, or to look at his growing corn, or at his grass-meadows, his heart would fill with joy. The grass that grew and the flowers that bloomed there seemed to him unlike any that grew elsewhere. Formerly, when he had passed by that land, it had appeared the same as any other land, but now it seemed quite different.

III

So Pahóm was well-contented, and everything would have been right if the neighboring peasants would only not have trespassed on his corn-fields and meadows. He appealed to them most civilly, but they still went on: now the Communal herdsmen would let the village cows stray into his meadows, then horses from the night pasture would get among his corn. Pahóm turned them out again and again, and forgave their owners, and for a long time he forbore to prosecute any one. But at last he lost patience and complained to the District Court. He knew it was the peasants' want of land, and no evil intent on their part, that caused the trouble, but he thought:

"I cannot go on overlooking it or they will destroy all I have. They must be taught a lesson."

So he had them up, gave them one lesson, and then another, and two or three of the peasants were fined. After a time Pahóm's neighbors began to bear him a grudge for this, and would now and then let their cattle on to his land on purpose. One peasant even got into Pahóm's wood at night and cut down five young lime trees for their bark. Pahóm passing through the wood one day noticed something white. He came nearer and saw the stripped trunks lying on the ground, and close by stood the stumps where the trees had been. Pahóm was furious.

"If he had only cut one here and there it would have been bad enough," thought Pahóm, "but the rascal has actually cut down a whole clump. If I could only find out who did this, I would pay him out."

He racked his brain as to who it could be. Finally he decided: "It must be Simon—no one else could have done it." So he went to Simon's homestead to have a look round, but he found nothing, and only had an angry scene. However, he now felt more certain than ever that Simon had done it, and he lodged a complaint. Simon was summoned. The case was tried, and retried, and at the end of it all Simon was acquitted, there being no evidence against him. Pahóm felt still more aggrieved, and let his anger loose upon the Elder and the Judges.

"You let thieves grease your palms," said he. "If you were honest folk yourselves you would not let a thief go free."

So Pahóm quarrelled with the Judges and with his neighbors. Threats to burn his buildings began to be uttered. So though Pahóm had more land, his place in the Commune was much worse than before.

About this time a rumor got about that many people were moving to new parts.

"There's no need for me to leave my land," thought Pahóm. "But some of the others might leave our village and then there would be more room for us. I would take over their land myself and make my estate a bit bigger. I could then live more at ease. As it is, I am still too cramped to be comfortable."

One day Pahóm was sitting at home when a peasant, passing through the village, happened to call in. He was allowed to stay the night, and supper was given him. Pahóm had a talk with this peasant and asked him where he came from. The stranger answered that he came from beyond the Vólga, where he had been working. One word led to another, and the man went on to say that many people were settling in those parts. He told how some people from his village had settled there. They had joined the Commune, and had had twenty-five acres per man granted them. The land was so good, he said, that the rye sown on it grew as high as a horse, and so thick that five cuts of a sickle made a sheaf. One peasant, he said, had brought nothing with him but his bare hands, and now he had six horses and two cows of his own.

Pahóm's heart kindled with desire. He thought:

"Why should I suffer in this narrow hole, if one

can live so well elsewhere? I will sell my land and my homestead here, and with the money I will start afresh over there and get everything new. In this crowded place one is always having trouble. But I must first go and find out all about it myself."

Towards summer he got ready and started. He went down the Vólga on a steamer to Samára, then walked another three hundred miles on foot, and at last reached the place. It was just as the stranger had said. The peasants had plenty of land: every man had twenty-five acres of Communal land given him for his use, and any one who had money could buy, besides, at a rúble an acre as much good freehold land as he wanted.

Having found out all he wished to know, Pahóm returned home as autumn came on, and began selling off his belongings. He sold his land at a profit, sold his homestead and all his cattle, and withdrew from membership in the Commune. He only waited till the spring, and then started with his family for the new settlement.

IV

As soon as Pahóm and his family reached their new abode, he applied for admission into the Commune of a large village. He stood treat to the Elders and obtained the necessary documents. Five shares of Communal land were given him for his own and his sons' use: that is to say—125 acres (not all together, but in different fields) besides the use of the Communal pasture. Pahóm put up the buildings he needed, and bought cattle. Of the Communal land alone he had three times as much as at his former home, and the land was good corn-land. He was ten times better off than he had been. He had plenty of arable land and pasturage, and could keep as many head of cattle as he liked.

At first, in the bustle of building and settling down,

Pahóm was pleased with it all, but when he got used to it he began to think that even here he had not enough land. The first year, he sowed wheat on his share of the Communal land and had a good crop. He wanted to go on sowing wheat, but had not enough Communal land for the purpose, and what he had already used was not available; for in those parts wheat is only sown on virgin soil or on fallow land. It is sown for one or two years, and then the land lies fallow till it is again overgrown with prairie grass. There were many who wanted such land and there was not enough for all; so that people quarreled about it. Those who were better off wanted it for growing wheat, and those who were poor wanted it to let to dealers, so that they might raise money to pay their taxes. Pahóm wanted to sow more wheat, so he rented land from a dealer for a year. He sowed much wheat and had a fine crop, but the land was too far from the village—the wheat had to be carted more than ten miles. After a time Pahóm noticed that some peasant-dealers were living on separate farms and were growing wealthy; and he thought:

"If I were to buy some freehold land and have a homestead on it, it would be a different thing altogether. Then it would all be nice and compact."

The question of buying freehold land recurred to him again and again.

He went on in the same way for three years, renting land and sowing wheat. The seasons turned out well and the crops were good, so that he began to lay money by. He might have gone on living contentedly, but he grew tired of having to rent other people's land every year, and having to scramble for it. Whereever there was good land to be had, the peasants would rush for it and it was taken up at once, so that unless you were sharp about it you got none. It happened in the third year that he and a dealer together rented a piece of pasture-land from some peasants; and they had already ploughed it up, when there was some dispute and the peasants went to law about it, and things fell out so that the labor was all lost.

"If it were my own land," thought Pahóm, "I should be independent, and there would not be all this unpleasantness."

So Pahóm began looking out for land which he could buy; and he came across a peasant who had bought thirteen hundred acres, but having got into difficulties was willing to sell again cheap. Pahóm bargained and haggled with him, and at last they settled the price at 1,500 rúbles, part in cash and part to be paid later. They had all but clinched the matter when a passing dealer happened to stop at Pahóm's one day to get a feed for his horses. He drank tea with Pahóm and they had a talk. The dealer said that he was just returning from the land of the Bashkírs, far away, where he had bought thirteen thousand acres of land, all for 1,000 rúbles. Pahóm questioned him further, and the tradesman said:

"All one need do is to make friends with the chiefs. I gave away about one hundred rúbles' worth of silk robes and carpets, besides a case of tea, and I gave wine to those who would drink it: and I got the land for less than a penny an acre." And he showed Pahóm the title-deeds, saying:

"The land lies near a river, and the whole prairie is virgin soil."

Pahóm plied him with questions, and the tradesman said:

"There is more land there than you could cover if you walked a year, and it all belongs to the Bashkírs. They are as simple as sheep, and land can be got almost for nothing."

"There now," thought Pahóm, "with my one thousand rúbles, why should I get only thirteen hundred acres, and saddle myself with a debt besides? If I take it out there, I can get more than ten times as much for the money."

V

Pahóm inquired how to get to the place, and as soon as the tradesman had left him, he prepared to go there himself. He left his wife to look after the homestead, and started on his journey taking his man with him. They stopped at a town on their way and bought a case of tea, some wine, and other presents, as the tradesman had advised. On and on they went until they had gone more than three hundred miles, and on the seventh day they came to a place where the Bashkírs had pitched their tents. It was all just as the tradesman had said. The people lived on the steppes, by a river, in felt-covered tents. They neither tilled the ground, nor ate bread. Their cattle and horses grazed in herds on the steppe. The colts were tethered behind the tents, and the mares were driven to them twice a day. The mares were milked, and from the milk kumiss was made. It was the women who prepared kumiss, and they also made cheese. As far as the men were concerned, drinking kumiss and tea, eating mutton, and playing on their pipes, was all they cared about. They were all stout and merry, and all the summer long they never thought of doing any work. They were quite ignorant, and knew no Russian, but were good-natured enough.

As soon as they saw Pahóm, they came out of their tents and gathered round their visitor. An interpreter was found, and Pahóm told them he had come about some land. The Bashkírs seemed very glad; they took Pahóm and led him into one of the best tents, where they made him sit on some down cushions placed on a carpet, while they sat round him. They gave him some tea and kumiss, and had a sheep killed, and gave him mutton to eat. Pahóm took presents out of his cart and distributed them among the Bashkírs, and divided the tea amongst them. The Bashkírs were delighted. They talked a great deal among themselves, and then told the interpreter to translate.

"They wish to tell you," said the interpreter, "that they like you, and that it is our custom to do all we can to please a guest and to repay him for his gifts. You have given us presents, now tell us which of the things we possess please you best, that we may present them to you."

"What pleases me best here," answered Pahóm, "is your land. Our land is crowded and the soil is exhausted; but you have plenty of land and it is good land. I never saw the like of it."

The interpreter translated. The Bashkírs talked among themselves for a while. Pahóm could not understand what they were saying, but saw that they were much amused and that they shouted and laughed. Then they were silent and looked at Pahóm while the interpreter said:

"They wish me to tell you that in return for your presents they will gladly give you as much land as you want. You have only to point it out with your hand and it is yours."

The Bashkírs talked again for a while and began to dispute. Pahóm asked what they were disputing about, and the interpreter told him that some of them thought they ought to ask their Chief about the land and not act in his absence, while others thought there was no need to wait for his return.

VI

While the Bashkírs were disputing, a man in a large fox-fur cap appeared on the scene. They all became silent and rose to their feet. The interpreter said, "This is our Chief himself."

Pahóm immediately fetched the best dressing-gown and five pounds of tea, and offered these to the Chief. The Chief accepted them, and seated himself in the place of honor. The Bashkírs at once began telling him something. The Chief listened for a while, then made a sign with his head for them to be silent, and addressing himself to Pahóm, said in Russian:

"Well, let it be so. Choose whatever piece of land you like; we have plenty of it."

"How can I take as much as I like?" thought Pahóm. "I must get a deed to make it secure, or else they may say, 'It is yours,' and afterwards may take it away again."

"Thank you for your kind words," he said aloud. "You have much land, and I only want a little. But I should like to be sure which bit is mine. Could it not be measured and made over to me? Life and death are in God's hands. You good people give it to me, but your children might wish to take it away again."

"You are quite right," said the Chief. "We will make it over to you."

"I heard that a dealer had been here," continued Pahóm, "and that you gave him a little land, too, and signed title-deeds to that effect. I should like to have it done in the same way."

The Chief understood.

"Yes," replied he, "that can be done quite easily. We have a scribe, and we will go to town with you and have the deed properly sealed."

"And what will be the price?" asked Pahóm.

"Our price is always the same: one thousand rúbles a day."

Pahóm did not understand.

"A day? What measure is that? How many acres would that be?"

"We do not know how to reckon it out," said the Chief. "We sell it by the day. As much as you can go round on your feet in a day is yours, and the price is one thousand rúbles a day."

Pahóm was surprised.

"But in a day you can get round a large tract of land," he said.

The Chief laughed.

"It will all be yours!" said he. "But there is one condition: If you don't return on the same day to the spot whence you started, your money is lost."

"But how am I to mark the way that I have gone?"

"Why, we shall go to any spot you like, and stay there. You must start from that spot and make your round, taking a spade with you. Wherever you think necessary, make a mark. At every turning, dig a hole and pile up the turf; then afterwards we will go round with a plough from hole to hole. You may make as large a circuit as you please, but before the sun sets you must return to the place you started from. All the land you cover will be yours."

Pahóm was delighted. It was decided to start early next morning. They talked a while, and after drinking some more kumiss and eating some more mutton, they had tea again, and then the night came on. They gave Pahóm a feather-bed to sleep on, and the Bashkírs dispersed for the night, promising to assemble the next morning at daybreak and ride out before sunrise to the appointed spot.

VII

Pahóm lay on the feather-bed, but could not sleep. He kept thinking about the land.

"What a large tract I will mark off!" thought he. "I can easily do thirty-five miles in a day. The days are long now, and within a circuit of thirty-five miles what a lot of land there will be! I will sell the poorer land, or let it to peasants, but I'll pick out the best and farm it. I will buy two oxteams, and hire two more laborers. About a hundred and fifty acres shall be ploughland, and I will pasture cattle on the rest."

Pahóm lay awake all night, and dozed off only just before dawn. Hardly were his eyes closed when he had a dream. He thought he was lying in that same tent and heard somebody chuckling outside. He wondered who it could be, and rose and went out, and he saw the Bashkír Chief sitting in front of the tent holding his sides and rolling about with laughter. Going nearer to the Chief, Pahóm asked: "What are you laughing at?" But he saw that it was no longer the Chief, but the dealer who had recently stopped at his house and had told him about the land. Just as Pahóm was going to ask, "Have you been here long?" he saw that it was not the dealer, but the peasant who had come up from the Vólga, long ago, to Pahóm's old home. Then he saw that it was not the peasant either, but the Devil himself with hoofs and horns, sitting there and chuckling, and before him lay a man barefoot, prostrate on the ground, with only trousers and a shirt on. And Pahóm dreamt that he looked more attentively to see what sort of a man it was that was lying there, and he saw that the man was dead, and that it was himself! He awoke horror-struck.

"What things one does dream," thought he.

Looking round he saw through the open door that the dawn was breaking.

"It's time to wake them up," thought he. "We ought to be staring."

He got up, roused his man (who was sleeping in his cart), bade him harness; and went to call the Bashkírs.

"It's time to go to the steppe to measure the land," he said.

The Bashkírs rose and assembled, and the Chief came too. Then they began drinking kumiss again, and offered Pahóm some tea, but he would not wait.

"If we are to go, let us go. It is high time," said he.

VIII

The Bashkírs got ready and they all started: some mounted on horses, and some in carts. Pahóm drove in his own small cart with his servant and took a spade with him. When they reached the steppe, the morning red was beginning to kindle. They ascended a hillock (called by the Bashkírs a *shikhan*) and dismounting from their carts and their horses, gathered in one spot. The Chief came up to Pahóm and stretching out his arm towards the plain:

"See," said he, "all this, as far as your eye can reach, is ours. You may have any part of it you like."

Pahóm's eyes glistened: it was all virgin soil, as flat as the palm of your hand, as black as the seed of a poppy, and in the hollows different kinds of grasses grew breast high.

The Chief took off his fox-fur cap, placed it on the ground and said:

"This will be the mark. Start from here, and return here again. All the land you go round shall be yours."

Pahóm took out his money and put it on the cap. Then he took off his outer coat, remaining in his sleeveless under-coat. He unfastened his girdle and tied it tight below his stomach, put a little bag of bread into the breast of his coat, and tying a flask of water to his girdle, he drew up the tops of his boots, took the spade from his man, and stood ready to start. He considered for some moments which way he had better go—it was tempting everywhere."No matter," he concluded, "I will go towards the rising sun."

He turned his face to the east, stretched himself, and waited for the sun to appear above the rim.

"I must lose no time," he thought, "and it is easier walking while it is still cool."

The sun's rays had hardly flashed above the horizon, before Pahóm, carrying the spade over his shoulder, went down into the steppe.

Pahóm started walking neither slowly nor quickly. After having gone a thousand yards he stopped, dug a hole, and placed pieces of turf one on another to make it more visible. Then he went on; and now that he had walked off his stiffness he quickened his pace. After a while he dug another hole.

Pahóm looked back. The hillock could be distinctly seen in the sunlight, with the people on it, and the glittering tires of the cart-wheels. At a rough guess Pahóm concluded that he had walked three miles. It was growing warmer; he took off his undercoat, flung it across his shoulder, and went on again. It had grown quite warm now; he looked at the sun, it was time to think of breakfast.

"The first shift is done, but there are four in a day, and it is too soon yet to turn. But I will just take off my boots," said he to himself.

He sat down, took off his boots, stuck them into his girdle, and went on. It was easy walking now.

"I will go on for another three miles," thought he, "and then turn to the left. The spot is so fine, that it would be a pity to lose it. The further one goes, the better the land seems."

He went straight on for a while, and when he looked round, the hillock was scarcely visible and the people on it looked like black ants, and he could just see something glistening there in the sun.

"Ah," thought Pahóm, "I have gone far enough in this direction, it is time to turn. Besides I am in a regular sweat, and very thirsty."

He stopped, dug a large hole, and heaped up pieces of turf. Next he untied his flask, had a drink, and then turned sharply to the left. He went on and on; the grass was high, and it was very hot.

Pahóm began to grow tired: he looked at the sun and saw that it was noon.

"Well," he thought, "I must have a rest."

He sat down, and ate some bread and drank some water; but he did not lie down, thinking that if he did he might fall asleep. After sitting a little while, he went on again. At first he walked easily: the food had strengthened him; but it had become terribly hot and he felt sleepy, still he went on, thinking: "An hour to suffer, a life-time to live."

He went a long way in this direction also, and was about to turn to the left again, when he perceived a damp hollow: "It would be a pity to leave that out," he thought. "Flax would do well there." So he went on past the hollow, and dug a hole on the other side of it before he turned the corner. Pahóm looked towards the hillock. The heat made the air hazy: it seemed to be quivering, and through the haze the people on the hillock could scarcely be seen.

"Ah!" thought Pahóm, "I have made the sides too long; I must make this one shorter." And he went along the third side, stepping faster. He looked at the sun: it was nearly half-way to the horizon, and he had not yet done two miles of the third side of the square. He was still ten miles from the goal.

"No," he thought, "though it will make my land lop-sided, I must hurry back in a straight line now. I might go too far, and as it is I have a great deal of land."

So Pahóm hurriedly dug a hole, and turned straight towards the hillock.

IX

Pahóm went straight towards the hillock, but he now walked with difficulty. He was done up with the heat, his bare feet were cut and bruised, and his legs began to fail. He longed to rest, but it was impossible if he meant to get back before sunset. The sun waits for no man, and it was sinking lower and lower.

"Oh dear," he thought, "if only I have not

blundered trying for too much! What if I am too late?"

He looked towards the hillock and at the sun. He was still far from his goal, and the sun was already near the rim.

Pahóm walked on and on; it was very hard walking but he went quicker and quicker. He pressed on, but was still far from the place. He began running, threw away his coat, his boots, his flask, and his cap, and kept only the spade which he used as a support.

"What shall I do," he thought again, "I have grasped too much and ruined the whole affair. I can't get there before the sun sets."

And this fear made him still more breathless. Pahóm went on running, his soaking shirt and trousers stuck to him and his mouth was parched. His breast was working like a blacksmith's bellows, his heart was beating like a hammer, and his legs were giving way as if they did not belong to him. Pahóm was seized with terror lest he should die of the strain.

Though afraid of death, he could not stop. "After having run all that way they will call me a fool if I stop now," thought he. And he ran on and on, and drew near and heard the Bashkírs yelling and shouting to him, and their cries inflamed his heart still more. He gathered his last strength and ran on.

The sun was close to the rim, and cloaked in mist looked large, and red as blood. Now, yes now, it was about to set! The sun was quite low, but he was also quite near his aim. Pahóm could already see the people on the hillock waving their arms to hurry him up. He could see the fox-fur cap on the ground and the money on it, and the Chief sitting on the ground holding his sides. And Pahóm remembered his dream.

"There is plenty of land," thought he, "but will God let me live on it? I have lost my life, I have lost my life! I shall never reach that spot!"

Pahóm looked at the sun, which had reached the earth: one side of it had already disappeared. With all his remaining strength he rushed on, bending his body forward so that his legs could hardly follow fast enough to keep from falling. Just as he reached the hillock it suddenly grew dark. He looked up—the sun had already set! He gave a cry: "All my labor has been in vain," thought he, and was about to stop, but he heard the Bashkírs still shouting, and remembered that though to him, from below, the sun seemed to have set, they on the hillock could still see it. He took a long breath and ran up the hillock. It was still light there. He reached the top and saw the cap. Before it sat the Chief laughing and holding his sides. Again Pahóm remembered his dream, and he uttered a cry: his legs gave way beneath him, he fell forward and reached the cap with his hands.

"Ah, that's a fine fellow!" exclaimed the Chief. "He has gained much land!"

Pahóm's servant came running up and tried to raise him, but he saw that blood was flowing from his mouth. Pahóm was dead!

The Bashkírs clicked their tongues to show their pity.

His servant picked up the spade and dug a grave long enough for Pahóm to lie in, and buried him in it. Six feet from his head to his heels was all he needed.